Beyond Total Quality Manage

LARRY REYNOLDS is a management
consultant. He works with a variety of
organizations in the private, public and social
welfare sectors, helping them to manage difficult
changes effectively. Work, learning, family and
friends all play an important part in his life, and he
works hard to find the right balance between them.
Larry lives in Yorkshire, and is married with one
daughter.

Sheldon Business Books

Sheldon Business Books is a list which exists to promote and facilitate the adoption of humane values and equal opportunities integrated with the technical and commercial expertise essential for successful business practice. Both practical and theoretical issues which challenge today's workforce will be explored in jargon-free, soundly researched books.

The first titles in the series are:
Making Change Work for You
by Alison Hardingham
Taking the Macho Out of Management
by Paddy O'Brien
How to Succeed in Psychometric Tests by David Cohen
Fit to Work by Paddy O'Brien

Larry Reynolds **Beyond Total Quality Management**

Sheldon Business Books

sheldon PRESS

First published in Great Britain 1994
Sheldon Press, SPCK, Marylebone Road, London NW1 4DU

© Larry Reynolds 1994

British Library Cataloguing-in-Publication Data
A catalogue record for this book is available from the British
Library
ISBN 0-85969-675-8

Photoset by Deltatype Ltd, Ellesmere Port, Cheshire
Printed in Great Britain at the University Press, Cambridge

To Len and Eve

Contents

Acknowledgements

I'd like to thank everyone who contributed to this book: to all the people who agreed to be interviewed as part of the initial research; to Paddy O'Brien, who first suggested that I write a book on quality; to Joanna Moriarty at Sheldon Press who taught me that it was possible; and to my wife Monica, who endured my anti-social behaviour while writing it.

Larry Reynolds, April 1993

Introduction

All of us would like quality in our lives. When we buy new clothes we want them to feel and look good. If we travel by public transport, we want to have a pleasant journey and arrive on time. If we need to go to hospital we want to be attended to promptly by knowledgeable and friendly staff. If we go for a night out at the cinema or theatre we want to enjoy the show with no technical hitches and we want to feel comfortable in the surroundings. Sadly, there is often a big gap between the quality we would like and the quality we receive. All of us have stories to tell of when things went really wrong: the train that was three hours late; the new washing machine which flooded the kitchen the first time we used it. Stories of mere mediocre quality are commonplace. Why is there this gap between what we would like and what organizations seem able to provide? More importantly, what can be done to improve things? That is the subject of this book. Total Quality Management (TQM) is an approach to developing organizations so that they not only meet customer expectations but actually exceed them. TQM has been applied in thousands of organizations around the world – not only in business but in local government, public services and even charities. Many of these organizations have achieved tremendous results through TQM; the current worldwide success of Japanese motor and electronics industries is largely due to using TQM techniques. On the other hand many organizations – especially in Britain – have found TQM difficult to apply.

There are at least two hundred books currently on the market dealing with TQM, so why add another one to the list? Most books explain the techniques of TQM and give examples of how they have been successfully used in different settings; this book will be no exception. What I then go on to do is to look at some of the circumstances where TQM has failed, or would be unsuitable. The idea is to present a more balanced picture of TQM in such a way that allows the reader to make up his or her mind about what is useful and what is merely exaggeration and hype. In particular, I give a lot of attention to the difficulties of implementing TQM. Like most approaches to management, the concepts are relatively straightforward; implementing them in real organizations is extremely tricky.

TQM was originally developed in a manufacturing setting, and so it is unsurprising that many books are written from this point of view. However, the concepts of TQM are being increasingly applied to bodies which provide services, whether in the private, public or voluntary sector. There are many useful lessons to be learnt from comparing similarities and differences between types of organization. In this book I will illustrate the concepts of TQM with examples taken from a wide range of organizations, including theatres, hospitals, charities, public transport, and oil companies, as well as manufacturing industry.

This book will also consider the ethical side of Total Quality Management. If used well, TQM is a highly moral approach to developing organizations and individuals. It places high value on honesty, integrity and co-operation. Despite this, there are aspects of TQM which some people feel uneasy about; for example, it is said that TQM is just another management device for controlling the workers. These ethical questions will be examined in the later chapters of the book.

There is no doubt that quality will be increasingly important to all organizations, and that the techniques of TQM will have an enduring relevance in many different settings. The techniques will be refined and developed. This book looks to the future of quality in organizations, not only at TQM but beyond. First, we must begin with TQM as it is now.

I What is Total Quality Management?

In researching this book, I interviewed people in some forty organizations involved in some way in Total Quality Management (TQM). Here is a selection of their comments.

TQM has transformed this organization. We used to be a very ordinary, second-rate regional theatre. By systematically applying TQM over the last three years, we've transformed the place into one of the best, if not the best regional theatre in the country.

Theatre general manager

Working in the storeroom used to be the pits – morale was non-existent and everyone else in the company treated us like dirt. Then a new head storekeeper arrived. He's obsessed by two things – giving our customers what they want and measurement. Everywhere you look now in the stores there are charts recording how we've improved our service to customers that week. He's really turned around the morale – it's a brilliant place to work now.

Stores worker, manufacturing company

As a fairly small national charity we were in danger of being swamped by a much larger charity working in the same field. We decided to put a very modest investment of time and money into developing a Quality Assurance system. We rely on local authorities for most of our grants and increasingly they want to see some kind of Quality Assurance procedure before they'll release any money. The QA system has been very successful and has benefited us in a number of ways. We now get a lot more positive feedback from our clients and this has led to a big improvement in staff morale – everyone is much more purposeful about their jobs now.

Charity treasurer

I was very sceptical about TQM at first. We were all working as hard as we could in the finance department, and it was difficult to see how we could make any improvements without extra staff – and we knew that wasn't an option. Despite my misgivings I agreed to take part in a cross-departmental quality improvement group. This included people from the operational departments as well as from different sections within finance itself. Although the first few meetings were quite difficult it turned out to be a great idea. The project has led to some dramatic improvements in the finance department – we can now turn an invoice around in 10 days not 20 and our error rate has dropped from 20% to under 5%.

Local authority finance officer

Not all the respondents were this enthusiastic.

Our chief executive introduced TQM. He insisted that it was vital to our company's survival, and brought in consultants to run a two-day seminar for senior staff – 'to ensure our commitment from the word go', as he put it. We reacted in different ways to the seminar – I could see that there was a lot of merit in what the consultants were saying, but a number of my colleagues felt quite insulted; they felt they were already working flat out and it was as if they were being told that it wasn't good enough. However, one incident really killed the whole thing. The consultants had just done a session on problem solving, and how important it was for managers to listen to staff. Then the chief executive did his session. A few of us were very open with him about our concerns both with TQM and with the company's general direction. He didn't seem to listen to any of our objections – he just went on about what a good thing TQM was. Within the month the whole TQM initiative was quietly abandoned.

Marketing director, financial services company

The bosses upstairs make a big song and dance about quality. Every Tuesday we close the shop for half an hour to do staff training, and these days that usually means videos about quality and customer service. I don't think it makes any difference to how we deal with the general public – that's largely good manners and common sense anyway – but it's nice to have a sit down and a chat. The rest of the day we're on our feet the whole time.

Shop assistant, high street retailer

The director is very keen on quality. We've just had consultants in to look at every aspect of the department's operations. Everything everyone does has been recorded in minute detail and this has been submitted to the British Standards Institution. The idea is that they will grant us BS 5750 and we can then say what a quality organization we are. Personally I think it's been a big waste of time and money. I don't think the service we provide to clients has improved one jot. If anything, having all these written procedures will stop us from bringing about real organizational change, and that's badly needed in the current climate.

Local authority training officer

Total Quality Management can be a huge success, and it can also be a huge flop. Other research paints a similar picture. A team from Durham University studied 235 firms in the north of England who had implemented some kind of quality programme. They concluded that while some companies did benefit from improved performance, better staff attitudes and customer satisfaction, most put too much emphasis on internal matters. They were not concerned enough about what customers want – the very opposite of what quality programmes are supposed to be about. Similar in tone was a recent report from Ashridge Management School, which studied 50 companies throughout Europe. In a majority of cases TQM consisted mainly of training courses added on to existing jobs. At best they were ineffective, at worst they prevented real change. In the few companies which genuinely integrated quality into the fabric of the business, however, there were measurable benefits in profitability and competitiveness.

The success or otherwise of Total Quality Management (TQM) depends very much on how it is implemented, and this thorny issue will be discussed in detail later. First we must look at what TQM actually is, beginning with the concept of quality itself.

What is quality?

When we say that a piece of music has a certain quality, we are using the word to describe characteristics which are not easily measured or quantified. The word quality is often used in this way: we talk of the quality of our drinking water, the quality of education at our local secondary school, even the quality of life itself. The word is also used, in a slightly different way, to describe something which is 'upmarket' or 'top of the range'. A Rolls Royce is a quality car; an expensive French bistro is a quality restaurant.

In the TQM sense, however, the word quality is used a little differently again. It is defined in terms of meeting the needs of the user. For a family living on a remote hillside farm at the end of a very bumpy track, their transport needs might best be met by an old but reliable Land Rover. In this context a Land Rover is a quality car and a Rolls Royce is not. For someone who enjoys a quick meal of burger and chips, McDonalds is a quality restaurant; an expensive French bistro is not. So far as TQM is concerned, quality, like beauty, is very much in the eye of the beholder; for me quality clothing might be a comfortable if somewhat threadbare old pullover; for you it might be a smart business suit. Quality is defined very much in terms of what the user wants and expects. In TQM terms, quality need not be expensive. If a customer wants a distinctive, hand-knit designer pullover she may have to pay over a hundred pounds for it. But if she wants something cheap and cheerful to keep her warm while decorating the garage she might be happy with a second-hand jumper bought at a car boot sale for £1. Both are quality products if they meet her needs.

The quality of any particular product or service is composed of many separate elements. The quality of a loaf of bread depends not only on its taste and physical appearance, but also its perceived and actual nutritional value, how long it keeps and perhaps even on the way it is displayed and sold. The quality of service provided by a hospital will be composed of dozens if not hundreds of variables: the appearance of the wards and waiting rooms, the length of time people must wait to receive attention, the general willingness of staff to be helpful, the expertise of both medical and administrative staff and their ability to respond to each patient as an individual – to mention but a few.

Apart from the word 'quality' itself, the most commonly used word in TQM is 'customer'. As with quality, the meaning is not quite the everyday one. Anyone who is supplied with a service or with a product is a customer. Passengers are the customers of a bus service, patients are customers of a hospital and we are all customers of the police in that they provide us with a law enforcement service.

Why is quality important? In the private sector the answer is fairly obvious: if a rival company can deliver better quality at the same price, sooner or later customers will catch on and take their custom elsewhere. As British Caledonian, the airline company, used to say, 'We always remember you have a choice'. (Unfortunately too many of their customers exercised that choice, and falling levels of demand eventually led to their takeover by British Airways.) In the public and voluntary sectors users of services often do not have a choice. In the past this has led to some public bodies appearing to be run for their own convenience, rather than for the benefit of anyone else. Some years ago I complained to my local bus company that I'd seen an almost empty bus driving past a long queue of passengers who were waiting at a bus stop. It was explained to me that this was sometimes necessary if the buses were to keep to the timetable at busy times. This attitude is fast disappearing. Public transport bodies are now much more interested in providing a quality service, that is, one which meets the needs of its passengers. A similar change is taking place in public services of all kinds: schools, hospitals, libraries, government departments, local authorities. Most people would agree there is still a long way to go. TQM can provide these kinds of organizations with a very powerful tool to bring about the kind of changes that are needed.

Although the TQM definition of quality is a very useful one, there are some difficulties in using it. The first difficulty is this: is quality what the customer would like or what they expect? I would like a train service which transports me instantaneously between any two points in the country; I know this is not realistic, but I certainly expect trains to be reasonably swift and to run on time. TQM aims to meet customer expectations, and where possible exceed them. Moreover these expectations are constantly increasing. Five years ago I was satisfied with a train journey from London to Leeds which lasted three hours. Now I expect it to last only two. TQM recognizes that customer expectations will usually increase over time, and it is therefore a philosophy of continuous improvement. TQM itself is a journey, not a destination.

A second difficulty with quality is defining it precisely in particular circumstances. What constitutes a quality train service? Some aspects are easy to define: trains which run reliably to time. If you wished to be more precise you could say trains which are never more than ten minutes late, and which are up to ten minutes late less than five per cent of the time. Other aspects of a quality train service are more problematic. For many people, a quality train service includes trains which are clean and comfortable. How can this be specified? Since one meaning of the word is that quality is anything non-quantitive, this at first sight presents a problem. However, one of the key aspects of quality in the TQM sense is that you must be able to measure it. So train cleanliness might be measured by the amount of litter on the seats and floor at any given time, or by means of passenger responses to a survey, or by how often the train is cleaned. The precise measures can be debated, but what is vital is that some agreed measures are found.

Since customers are so important in the TQM definition of quality, it is tempting to think that quality can somehow be added on at the last minute before the customer receives the product or service. Over the last few years, all British Rail staff have been through an intensive customer-care training programme. My experience of travelling by train is almost always that staff are polite and helpful. Unfortunately, my experience is often that trains are late; although I appreciate being told why in a helpful and polite way, no amount of this will compensate for the fact that my train is late and that by my definition I am not receiving a quality service. To understand why the train is late it is necessary to delve far back into the organization of British Rail. The quality of a service cannot be added on at the last minute by customer-care training. Equally the quality of a product cannot be added on at the last minute as it rolls off the production line.

To produce a genuine quality product or service, quality must be built in at the very start and maintained at every stage. TQM provides a very powerful tool for doing this: the concept of customer–supplier chains.

Customer–supplier chains

If I go into a shop and buy a bar of chocolate, I become one of the shop's customers. The shop itself is a customer of the manufacturing firm which supplies it. Going a step further back down the chain, the manufacturers are supplied with raw materials from (amongst other places) a cocoa farm in West Africa. The manufacturers are customers of the cocoa farm. There is a complete chain of customers and suppliers linking the cocoa farm to me, the final customer in the chain.

Fig. 1

TQM goes one step further. As well as looking at customer–supplier chains *between* different organizations, it is useful to consider them *within* organizations. A simplified model of the chocolate manufacturing company would look like figure 2.

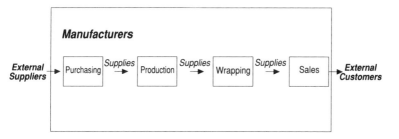

Fig. 2

The purchasing department buys raw materials from outside the company and supplies them to its internal customer, the production department. This department turns the sugar, milk, cocoa beans and all the rest into bars of chocolate. The production department supplies this newly made chocolate to its internal customer, the wrapping department. When the chocolate bars are wrapped they become the responsibility of the sales department. The sales people are the only department to have contact with external customers.

Although this is a simplified example, customer–supplier chains in manufacturing companies are often comparatively straightforward. In other types of organizations they can be more complex. In figure 3 there is a simplified customer–

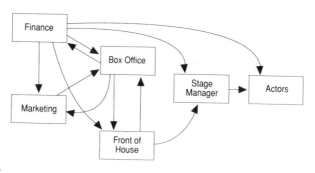

Fig. 3

supplier chain for a theatre. Each arrow points from a supplier to a customer. So for example the box office supplies the finance department with details of each evening's takings. The finance department supplies the marketing department with accurate information on the income from each performance so that it can plan its marketing strategy. The marketing department supplies the box office with a resumé of each play so that box office staff can better respond to enquiries from potential playgoers. In this case the customer–supplier chain is more of a net than a chain. Many of the ideas of TQM were first developed in a manufacturing setting, where customer–supplier chains are often linear in nature. In most other settings, they are in reality more like nets, webs or tangles.

From Quality Control to TQM

How is the customer–supplier chain concept used in TQM? Let us return to the chocolate factory. What would happen if the wrapping department supplied chocolate bars to the sales department in wrappers which were badly printed? If the next time I buy chocolate the label is blurred, then I am no longer receiving a quality product; for me a quality chocolate bar tastes good and is attractively and hygienically wrapped. Apart from anything else, if the label is wrong it might lead me to think that the chocolate itself hasn't been made properly, and this gives me another reason for choosing a rival brand next time.

One way of avoiding this situation is to employ examiners to check chocolate bars before they leave the factory. If they notice any badly wrapped bars they are removed before they are sent to the wholesalers. These duds may be simply thrown away, or sent back to the wrapping department to be wrapped again. While this system of *Quality Control* is better than no system at all, it is a very poor way of ensuring quality. There are the additional salary costs of each examiner. Whether the dud chocolate bars are thrown away or rewrapped, it costs more money. These extra costs must be passed on to the final customer. This process is therefore very wasteful and in the long run very expensive. Nevertheless it is still very common in British companies.

Another approach to this problem is known as *Quality Assurance.* When anything goes wrong in the customer–supplier chain, the first step is to find out why. In my example there could be dozens of reasons why the labels were badly printed: perhaps the printing machine was not adequately maintained; perhaps the wrong ink or the wrong paper were used; perhaps the person working the printing machine simply could not be bothered to make sure the labels were done properly; or perhaps he or she was new and hadn't been properly trained. Having discovered the reason, the next step is to remedy things so that the problem will never recur. This is easier said than done, but let's assume for now that the root cause has been identified and remedied. The next step is to write down the exact procedures necessary to ensure that these problems will not happen again. This is incorporated into the company's Quality Assurance manual – a detailed set of systems and procedures which ensures that quality is delivered to every customer in the customer–supplier chain, every time. In some cases organizations take their quality assurance manuals to the British Standards Institution (BSI). If the procedures in the Quality Assurance manual are validated by the BSI the organization is entitled to British Standard 5750. A number of organizations are very proud of their BS 5750 and use it on their promotional literature.

Many people confuse Quality Assurance with Total Quality Management but they are different. Quality Assurance is about reaching a certain level of quality, documenting the procedures and staying there. TQM, on the other hand, says that no level of quality is acceptable; there is always room for further improvement. Even if customers appear perfectly satisfied with current levels of quality, they will not be in the future; their expectations will increase, especially if other similar organizations can offer something better. Imagine an organization as a drum rolling up an incline towards ever greater levels of quality. TQM is the mechanism which drives it upwards; Quality Assurance is the wedge which stops it slipping back when a certain level has been achieved; Quality Control has long been left behind at the lowest level of quality.

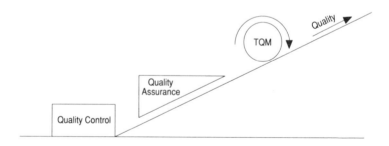

Fig. 4

The management of TQM

Although quality is very important, it is very elusive. Most of us have stories to tell of products we have purchased which have been damaged, didn't work, or failed to meet our expectations in some other way. The companies which supplied us with these products often add insult to injury by refusing to apologize for poor quality, or failing to offer any redress. I have particularly strong memories of finding a small caterpillar in a salad at a restaurant. When I complained the waiter told me I was making a lot of fuss over nothing. In these circumstances we are often left wondering how such places stay in business. When it comes to public services, the situation is even worse. In Britain, at least, we have almost come to accept poor service in public agencies. It is unfortunately no surprise to go to a hospital or an unemployment benefit office to find that you have to queue a long time before being poorly treated by staff.

What is clearly needed is some kind of system which enables organizations of all kinds to provide a better service to their customers, and this is exactly what TQM sets out to do. It is both a philosophy of management and set of techniques which can be applied to almost any organization to improve the quality of service that customers receive. In fact, TQM not only improves the quality, it reduces costs. Most organizations exist either to make money (as many private sector companies do), or to serve customers (as most public agencies do), or to do both. TQM therefore has something to offer all types of organizations. As the name Total Quality Management suggests, TQM is a management system: it is designed to be implemented by the people in organizations who co-ordinate, enable and control, rather than those who directly do the work. In this sense TQM is very much a 'top down' method for achieving organizational change, rather than a 'bottom up' one. This is not to say that TQM regards 'the workers' as unimportant; on the contrary TQM makes the assumption that most workers would do their best to provide a quality service to their customers were it not for the obstacles which get in the way. The task of managers, therefore, is to use TQM to remove these barriers to allow people to do a good job.

First of all, managers must be clear about what their organization is trying to achieve; to put this in TQM terms, who are the external customers and what do they want? In some organizations this is comparatively simple. To take the chocolate factory example, market research will quickly establish who buys chocolate bars and what they want in terms of taste, appearance and so on. For other organizations, however, it may be very difficult to say exactly who the customers are. Who are the customers of a school? Are they the pupils themselves, their parents, potential employers or the community as a whole? If we agree that all are customers in a sense, how do we resolve conflicting priorities? Parents may define the quality of a school by its ability to instil certain basic skills, whilst the pupils may be more interested in how friendly and fair the teachers are. Even if the school decides to focus on one set of customers – say, the parents – identifying exactly what constitutes quality remains difficult. One parent may define a quality school as one that values discipline and good manners; for another, academic performance may be the main criterion. For many organizations outside the commercial sector it is very awkward to define exactly who the customers are and what they want. However, it is extremely valuable to have the debate within the organization. This process of clarification can lead to an improvement in quality for everyone concerned.

Having established a common view of what the organization is trying to do in terms of external customers, the manager's next task is to look within the organization, to identify any areas within the customer–supplier chain where there is a lapse of quality. A secretary types a letter and gives it to her manager to sign. The manager points out that there are a couple of mistakes in the letter and asks her secretary to correct it. Since the secretary has been using a word processor, this takes only a moment. The amended letter is printed off, signed and put in the post, and the incorrect version is thrown in the bin. Since the manager notices such mistakes in perhaps only one in ten letters, she takes no further action.

Did the manager respond appropriately to this situation? Most managers would tolerate such a low 'failure rate'. However, TQM says that any failure rate is unacceptable. If only one letter in ten has to be thrown away like this, that is equivalent to taking every tenth delivery of stationery and putting it straight into the bin. To take a more extreme case, it is equivalent to asking a tenth of the secretaries working in the company to type meaningless rubbish while the other nine tenths produce good work. If the manager is committed to quality, her first step will be to analyse the reason for her secretary's mistake. This is not to say that she should merely blame the secretary for inattention. Instead the manager should work with the secretary to analyse the root cause – or causes – of the problem. It might be fatigue caused by poor working conditions, or perhaps the secretary did not fully understand the standards which were expected of her. It might be that she had not been trained to use the spelling checker supplied with her word processor. It might even be that the spelling checker installed on the software checks American spellings but not English ones. It might be the company is making redundancies and the secretary doesn't feel it is worth doing things well. It might be any one of a dozen other reasons. What all these reasons have in common is that they are barriers, which prevent the secretary from doing a good job – barriers which she is aware of but which only her manager (or more senior managers) have the power to remove. It is the manager's role first to work with the secretary to identify the barriers, and then to remove them.

When TQM is being introduced into an organization, people sometimes feel that this obsession with eliminating errors and getting things 'right first time' is somehow going too far. Surely everyone is human – we all make mistakes? Whilst it is true that all humans make mistakes, that is quite different to accepting a certain level of failure. Doctors are human but it is unacceptable for doctors to give the wrong treatment ten per cent of the time. Aircraft designers are human, but it is unacceptable for one per cent of aircraft to crash through design faults.

In some cases it is obvious where quality is lacking; the badly wrapped chocolate bars are one example. In other cases lapses of quality are so hidden, or so much accepted as part of everyday life, that it is sometimes difficult even to notice that they are there. The Royal Artillery is very proud of its displays of gunnery. A typical display begins with ten or more trucks towing field guns into an arena. As each truck pulls to a halt, six men leap out, unhook the field gun from the back of their truck, load it, aim it and fire it all within a matter of seconds. If you look closely during the display you will notice that only five of the team are really doing the work; the sixth jumps smartly out of the truck and stands to attention throughout. There is a good historical reason for this. In the days when field guns were horse drawn, the role of the sixth man was to hold the horse. Unfortunately many organizations have an equivalent of the sixth man – a system or a practice which once made sense but does no longer. TQM offers managers a number of techniques for identifying and eliminating waste and wasteful working practices. One of these is called a *quality improvement team (QIT)* and the following example illustrates one being used in the oil industry.

Contrary to popular belief, oil from the North Sea does not emerge onto the oil rig as a thick black treacle-like substance, but as a hot frothy liquid similar in appearance to Coca-Cola. It is very hot because it comes from deep below the earth's surface, and it is frothy because it is mixed with water from the rocks in which the oil lies. As this oil and water mixture emerges from the drilling pipe, it leaves a chalky deposit on the side of the pipe. The water is not pure, but contains a number of minerals, and what is happening is chemically very similar to the 'furring' which sometimes occurs inside kettles. In the early days of the North Sea oil industry there were relatively large quantities of oil to be exploited and no one was much bothered if the flow was somewhat reduced by a little furring. As North Sea oil begins to run out, and the relative costs of extraction increase, such problems become more serious. A chemical engineer in one major oil company calculated that this furring was costing his company several million pounds a year. Initially his findings were not taken very seriously by the company. Furring was accepted as a way of life. Even if it was costing the company a lot of money who knew how much more it might cost to fix? Eventually the engineer pursuaded his company to set up a quality improvement team.

A quality improvement team consists of representatives from different departments in an organization who get together for a fixed number of meetings to resolve a particular quality problem. This particular QIT consisted of chemical engineers, drillers, production people and finance staff. Over a six-month period the group gathered a great deal of data relating to the problem, analysed it, listened to presentations and submissions from relevant experts, and came up with over 100 different possible solutions to the problem. After further work and some practical testing the preferred solution was implemented. This involves injecting particular chemicals into the oil reservoir while it is being drained. Although both the QIT and the eventual solution cost a great deal of money, the improvement in oil production is saving the company several millions of pounds a year. Quality improvement teams are one of the techniques managers can use to improve quality in their organization. There are many others and they are described in more detail in chapter 3 of this book. However TQM is much more than just a set of tools and techniques – it is concerned with changing attitudes.

I recently ran a series of management courses for the staff of a university. The first set of courses was for academic staff. 'The university is a great place to work', I was told, 'but for one thing – the administrative staff. They can never organize the teaching rooms we need, or give us reliable information about students. To add insult to injury they're always asking us to fill in forms which so far as I'm concerned are a complete waste of time.' With few exceptions, a similar view was held by most of the academic staff at this particular institution. The next round of this training programme was for administrative staff. 'It would be a wonderful place to work except for the academic staff. We never get any thanks from them, only a string of complaints about things not done. Half the time it's their own fault because they don't give us the information we need to get things organized for them.' For each group of staff, the problems at the university were largely caused by the other group. Unfortunately, such interdepartmental hostility is not unusual; it is a feature of most organizations. Whether it is the marketing department slanging off the production department, the operations people insulting personnel, or everyone complaining about finance, it is common for much energy to go into hostility, rather than sorting things out for the benefit of the external customer.

This phenomenon of departmental rivalry is just one example of attitudes which prevent organizations improving quality. Perhaps more common is the notion of 'We've always done it this way'. Any suggestion of change is interpreted as criticism. Implementing TQM is much more than applying a set of techniques. It involves bringing about a fundamental change in the attitudes and behaviour of everyone in the organization, that is to say, a shift in organizational culture. This raises some interesting questions. Is it possible to bring about a change in organizational culture? A great deal of management training is based on the assumption that this can be done, and yet the evidence from real organizations is less convincing. Even if it is possible for a small group of managers to bring about cultural change in their organization, should they? It is sometimes argued that TQM is manipulative of employees, and puts too much emphasis on external customers at the expense of employees and suppliers. These and other dilemmas are explored later in this book.

2 Applying the Ideas

Having looked at the main principles of TQM in chapter 1, it is now time to see how they can be applied. If any organization is serious about TQM it must find answers to these six questions:

1 Who are our customers?
2 What do they expect?
3 What standard of service do we aim to provide?
4 How are we failing to do this?
5 Why are we failing to do this?
6 What can be done to improve things?

1 Who are our customers?

As we have already seen, answering this question may be very easy or very difficult. In the case of a chocolate manufacturer it is very straightforward to identify customers: they are the people who buy the chocolate bars. In the case of a school it may be much more complex: are the customers the pupils, their parents or the wider community? The level of difficulty in identifying customers largely depends on the type of organization, so we begin by examining the different characteristics of organizations in the private, public and social welfare sectors.

Private sector organizations – whether they are very large like British Gas, BP and ICI, or very small like my village shop – share one common characteristic: they have owners, who profit when things are going well and who bear the financial brunt when they are not. Private sector companies may have a very large number of owners in the form of shareholders, or they may be owned by a small group or even by just one person. In most cases, the profit motive has an important part to play in the way the organization is run; it is an important measure of success.

Most private sector companies generate their funds by trading, that is, by providing a product or service. A distinction is sometimes made between companies which make a product – cars, chocolate, or teaspoons – and those which provide a service – plumbing, legal advice, or consultancy. In TQM terms this is not a very helpful distinction since even product-based companies are in fact providing a service from the customer's point of view. The quality of a car depends not just on the physical product but also on the delivery time, the friendliness of the salesperson, the aftersales service and so on. Finally, most private sector companies experience some form of competition. Often this is very direct: if I don't like the food on offer at Sainsbury's I can go to Tesco's, or Safeway, or to Marks and Spencer, or to my local discount food store, or to my village shop. In other cases the competition is less direct: only one airline flies from Leeds to London and there is therefore no direct competition. However, there is indirect competition: I could drive, or take the train. In some circumstances I might simply decide not to go.

The profit motive, trading and competition are characteristics of most private sector companies. There are of course always exceptions to the rule. Co-operatives are set up not to make money but for other reasons, such as to provide employment. Some companies generate some or most of their funds not through trading but through investments. A few companies experience very little, if any competition – the privatized water companies, for example. However the vast majority of private sector companies do share these characteristics. Answering the question 'Who are our customers?' is therefore comparatively easy. They are the people who pay us for our services. For the chocolate factory it is the people who purchase confectionery, for a firm of plumbers it is the people who pay to have broken pipes mended and new bathrooms fitted.

For most of us, the services we require are provided not by private sector companies, but by public sector bodies like hospitals, libraries, schools and colleges, run by local or central government. Unlike the private sector, they do not have owners who profit from the services provided. They are not usually in competition. Most importantly, their funds are usually generated not by trading, but by taxation. The close link between users of the service and income, which is so critical to the functioning of a private sector company, is usually absent. Once again there are exceptions – a local authority housing department may be required to finance itself largely from tenants' rents – but the general pattern for the public sector is that income is derived from taxes, not trading. This separation of services and income leads to some difficulties in answering the question 'Who are our customers?' Are the customers of a housing department existing tenants or people who are homeless or in temporary accommodation? Are the customers of a social services department elderly people, people with mental health problems, children at risk? Are the customers of a hospital people requiring simple low cost operations or those needing expensive treatment? It is tempting to say that the answer should be all of these, but we then run into the problem of demand outstripping resources. A characteristic of many public sector services is that demand often outstrips supply. There are more people on waiting lists for council housing, hospital operations, and home help support than the relevant organizations are usually able to provide for.

The private sector is not usually faced with this problem. If demand outstrips supply, the private sector manager increases the price of the product or service. Customers select themselves on the basis of cost. The public sector manager cannot do this, as access to services is not usually determined by such market forces. Instead, managers in the public sector must take into account three sets of factors when deciding who their customers are, and what priority should be given to different groups.

The first of these is legislation. In a number of areas of the public sector, laws exist which effectively state what the priorities should be. For example, local authorities have a statutory duty to provide accommodation to homeless families. It would be illegal for a local authority to decide that the customers of the housing department were merely existing tenants, and that it wanted nothing to do with homeless people. A second source of guidance for public service managers is the concept of fairness. Local authorities often express this in terms of an equal opportunities statement: 'The local authority aims to provide services to all citizens of the borough irrespective of race, gender or disability.' However the concept of equal opportunities goes far beyond this. An important principle of public services such as health, education and housing is that they should be available to everyone. No one should be excluded, whether it is because they belong to a particular ethnic group, whether they have limited financial resources, or for any other unjust reason. The third factor to be considered is politics. Public sector managers are accountable to elected members of local or national government. These elected members will have views on the allocation of resources to public services; views based not only on specific electoral promises but also on personal preference. Public sector managers therefore have an extremely difficult job in deciding who the customers of their services should be; not only does demand outstrip resources, but they must juggle the (sometimes conflicting) guidance of legislation, equal opportunities and political intervention. Public sector managers are therefore faced with some genuine dilemmas in deciding who their customers are. While there can be no easy answers it is important to have the debate, so that each public sector organization is in a position to state honestly what it can and cannot do.

Finally there are an increasing number of organizations which are neither private nor public sector. They do not have owners, but they are independent of local and national government. This group includes universities, trust hospitals, many arts organizations, as well as charities and local groups such as tenants associations. I will refer to it as the social welfare sector. So far as TQM is concerned, the key characteristic of organizations in this sector is that the source of funds is often very removed from the services provided. Save the Children Fund (SCF) spends some £100m each year in a world-wide programme which includes famine relief, primary health care projects overseas and work with young offenders and prisoners' families in the UK. Funds for this work come from a variety or sources including individual donations, legacies, corporate giving, and local and national government grants. So who are SCF's customers? Not only are they the people receiving SCF's services, but also those providing money to the organization. It is vitally important to get the right balance between the various groups.

Arts organizations face similar quandaries about their customers. The Zone Gallery in Newcastle is a small photographic gallery with a national reputation for displaying fine photography. Who are its customers? Members of the public who come into the gallery by chance – perhaps to use the café – and decide to look at the photographs? People who travel great distances specifically to see an exhibition? The photographers themselves whose work is displayed? Or Northern Arts, the regional arts board whose annual grant keeps the gallery open?

In summary, the question 'Who are our customers?' becomes increasingly more difficult to answer as we move from private through public to social welfare sector organizations. However this is true only of external customers. If we use the concept of customer–supplier chains to look at internal customers, we find that even private sector organizations face exactly the same difficulties in defining customers as public and social welfare organizations. Consider the personnel department in the chocolate factory. It provides a welfare and counselling service to individual members of staff, it recruits new members of staff on behalf of managers, it negotiates with the trade union over salaries and working conditions. Its customers could be considered to be any of these groups of people, not to mention the board of directors who allocate a budget to the department to allow it to operate. For an organization or section within an organization to answer the question 'Who are our customers?' it must consider the related problem of 'What do they expect?'

2 What do they expect?

In TQM there are two golden rules when it comes to finding out what customers expect. The first is don't assume you already know. The second is find ways of measuring what customers expect.

It is important not to assume you know what customers expect, because these expectations are made up of a very complex set of factors. These include what they need from a service, what their past experience of this service has been – both from you and from comparable organizations – word-of-mouth communication they may have received about the service, and any communication or publicity your organization has put out. In some cases expectations may exceed personal needs, and in other cases the reverse may be true. A businesswoman may expect to be able to fly from London to Edinburgh in an hour, but she probably does not really need to be transported that quickly. On the other hand a homeless person clearly has a need for an adequate home, but she may not expect that the local authority will be able to provide her with one. Given this complexity, organizations frequently make the wrong assumptions both about what their customers would like and what they expect. It is therefore important to take specific actions to ensure that customer expectations are accurately identified. A Citizens' Advice Bureau undertook a quality initiative. As an early step the staff of the centre had an awayday at which they drew up a list of things they believed to be important to the people who came into the centre. Top of the list were convenient opening hours, friendly staff and a clean and tidy centre. As a check they asked one of their volunteers to interview a sample of people who used the centre about what they wanted. This list was quite different: top was privacy in discussing problems, followed by knowledgeable staff and a short waiting time. As a result of this survey a number of changes took place, including the provision of interview rooms in what had previously been a fairly open-plan space.

Japanese car companies can go to great lengths to find out exactly what people want from a car. One company conducted some very detailed market research using a technique called 'focus groups'. Small groups of existing and potential customers were invited to take part in fairly lengthy discussions about how they perceived quality in a car. Features like top speed were much less important than the way a person felt about the car when he or she stepped into it. One result of this research was that the doors of new models were designed to give exactly the right noise when they are shut – a clunk which gives the impression of safety and reliability.

The second golden rule concerns measurement. How can you measure what a customer wants? In some cases it is very easy. If I buy a battery for my radio I want it to last for a reasonable length of time, and I don't want it to leak. That's about it so far as batteries are concerned. In other cases it is much more difficult to measure what a customer expects. It would be more difficult for my GP to measure what I expect of a visit to her, partly because it involves a number of different elements – how friendly she is, how expert her advice, how long I must wait to see her and in what kind of surroundings – and partly because some of these elements are so difficult to pin down – how do you measure expertise or friendliness? In such cases it is necessary to use *performance indicators*, a series of measures which indicate whether quality is being delivered. A university lecturer identifies his customers as students. He is clear that what they want is high quality teaching. How does he measure this? The list of things which would indicate that high quality teaching was taking place includes:

- exam results
- student feedback
- feedback from other lecturers
- how popular the course was in terms of recruitment
- how many students got jobs as a result of the course.

This particular lecturer identifies three performance indicators which will be relevant in this case: exam results, student feedback (as gathered in an end-of-term questionnaire) and feedback from another lecturer (he will invite a colleague to observe one of his lectures). Taken together, these indicators will paint a fairly accurate picture of high quality teaching.

The use of performance indicators is becoming increasingly popular as a way of spelling out the level of service which an organization intends to provide as a way of meeting customer needs. If used sensitively it can be a very powerful tool. Unfortunately it is prone to misuse in a number of ways. First, performance indicators may focus too much on the wrong thing. The government publishes league tables of achievement in examinations for schools. As with the university lecturer, exam results are one way of assessing the quality of an educational service, but they can be misleading if they are taken as the only way. The whole point of performance indicators is that no single measure is adequate on its own; a range of measures (usually at least three) is needed to give a proper picture. Moreover, too much emphasis on one measure may actually result in the overall level of service going down. Schools which focus all their energies on preparing pupils for examinations will fail to provide the range of activities – inside and outside the classroom – which most people would consider necessary for a good education.

A second criticism of performance indicators is that too much energy goes into measurement and not enough into providing the service. If the university lecturer in my earlier example gathered data on all his performance indicators he would probably have little time left to prepare and deliver his lectures.

Despite these difficulties the use of performance indicators to measure customer satisfaction is extremely important in TQM. In the private sector there is usually one immediate measure of customer satisfaction: do customers come back for more? In the public and social welfare sectors this is not the case. Organizations can provide a very poor service, and yet customers are obliged to return because there is no alternative. Ironically it is often easier to provide a good service than a bad one, but organizations are simply not fully aware of what their customers want. When thoughtfully used, performance indicators can be a very effective way of measuring what customers want.

3 What standard of service do we aim to provide?

Organizations can rarely meet the expectations of all of their customers, and it would be dishonest of an organization to make this claim unless it were genuinely possible. Instead, organizations should aim to produce a clear statement of what they can deliver, and this statement should go as far as possible to meeting or exceeding customer expectations. Producing this statement involves consideration of three main areas:

- What does each group of customers expect of us?
- How do we prioritize the expectations of different groups when they are in conflict?
- What resources are available to us to provide these services, in terms of people, money, time, equipment and technology?

Here is an example of how a local authority housing department tackled these three questions. The director of housing initially spent a day with his three assistant directors developing a list of core values which they believed should inform the work of the whole department. This statement of values includes things like the right of tenants to an efficient service, and the right of staff not to be asked to work under undue pressure. Central to the list was the concept of equal opportunities: no tenant or staff member should receive unfair treatment on the grounds of race or gender. These core values were discussed, amended and agreed with the next tier of some thirty senior managers. These senior managers were then asked to prepare a list of key standards for their areas of responsibility: allocating tenancies, maintenance, caretaking, provision for homeless people, and so on. These key standards essentially listed the different groups of housing department customers and the level of service they expected. The director and his assistant directors drew these individual standards into one document. This was the most difficult part of the process. The senior managers had set ambitious standards for their sections, and yet resources were very limited. The council as a whole had been 'charge-capped' by central government; yet local councillors were not willing to see council rents increased. The director therefore had to make some difficult decisions as to which areas should receive which level of resourcing; in other words how to prioritize the needs of some groups against those of others. These decisions were made in the light of the core values which had already been agreed; so for example more resources were to be put into supporting caretaking staff, as this was one group which was currently working under very high levels of stress.

The draft list of standards which had been prepared by the director and his assistant directors was now the subject of very wide consultation. The director made a presentation about the document to every one of the department's 1,000 staff at a series of meetings in the various district housing offices. He listened carefully to the comments he received, some of which were very supportive and some very critical. These comments were incorporated into the final document. This final version consists of eighteen key standards. For example:

- We will reduce the number of homeless households in Bed and Breakfast accommodation to not more than 20.
- We will ensure that effective action is taken in response to any tenant who suffers nuisance or harassment.
- We will ensure that 95 per cent of emergency repairs are

carried out within 24 hours, and that all repairs are attended to within a week.

Each standard was broken down into a number of elements giving more detail of how it was to be achieved and how it was to be measured. Once the final document had been approved by staff, managers and councillors a version of it was produced for tenants. From start to finish the process had taken six months.

The biggest danger with this type of exercise is the tendency to overpromise. For private sector organizations there may be internal pressure – perhaps from the marketing department – to generate new business by making extravagant promises of service. Indeed there may be competition from competitors who are promising more than they can deliver. In the public sector the pressure is likely to be political. In the example given above, the director of housing felt strongly that if promises were to be made on the quality of the maintenance and repair service, then rents had to be increased to pay for this. He was overruled by the councillors on the housing committee who insisted on a higher maintenance standard and that rents should be pegged at existing levels. Perhaps unwittingly, they were ensuring that the council would fail on its promises for maintenance. There is nothing wrong with *aiming* for standards which may be difficult or even impossible to achieve; but it is important to distinguish between these aspirations and what is actually promised to customers.

4 How are we failing to reach the standard we have set ourselves?

It is clearly not sufficient merely to set standards for customer service; it is important to monitor whether they are being achieved. This often requires some formal kind of monitoring system. Each month the housing department described above publishes a staff bulletin explaining how the previous month's performance has matched up to standard. District housing managers discuss this bulletin with staff in order to remedy any discrepancies. Even if there is no formal monitoring system in place, there are a number of indications that quality service is not being provided. The most important of these is customer feedback, and in particular customer complaints. Most organizations would rather not hear customer complaints. Organizations which aspire to total quality make sure that complaints are not only heard, but passed to the most appropriate person to be dealt with.

Another indication of poor service is very long queues. There is a branch of mathematics called queuing theory, which examines the length of time a person is likely to wait in a queue given various parameters such as the average service time, the extent to which people arrive early or late if there is an appointment system and so on. In the past queuing theory has been used by organizations such as hospitals to ensure that whatever happens the doctor will not be left without a patient to see. The rationale for this is that it is inefficient to pay for a doctor who is not seeing a patient, but perfectly efficient to keep patients waiting, sometimes for hours. This assumes too narrow a view of an efficient service. From the customer's perspective the waiting time is one important measure of a quality service. Organizations need to ensure that queuing is kept to an acceptable minimum.

At first sight inspection and checking appears to be a sign of good quality; in fact the opposite is the case. Checking is certainly part of the Quality Control approach, but is not part of TQM. One local authority employs a parks maintenance team of twelve people, all working as effectively as possible. Another employs ten parks maintenance workers and two parks inspectors to check on their work. Which team provides the better service? Providing they really are performing as effectively as possible it will be the first group. Total Quality organizations concentrate on creating a climate where the work is done right first time, and does not require checking or redoing.

5 Why are we failing?

There are three reasons why an organization fails to deliver the service it has promised: external constraints, being let down by suppliers, and internal inefficiencies. Very occasionally external factors appear out of the blue and completely disrupt a service. A good example of this is the hurricane which struck the south of

England in October 1989. People are usually very understanding in these circumstances; few people complained that British Rail was unable to offer any kind of service on Network SouthEast on the following day. However, these kinds of unpredictable interruptions to service are very rare. Most external constraints can be predicted and it is the task of a quality organization to make those predictions. British Rail can reliably predict that leaves will fall from trees each autumn, and so it is not acceptable for them to blame poor service on 'leaves on the track'.

Most organizations are rarely troubled by external factors such as the weather, acts of terrorism and other unpredictable events. However all organizations, and especially those in the public and social welfare sectors, face one major constraint, that of financial resources. However efficient or effective an organization, resource constraints do limit its activities. Many London boroughs, for example, have seen a reduction in the provision of leisure services in recent years. Swimming pools which used to open for an early morning swim at 7 a.m. are now closed until 9 or even 10 a.m. This is not because the pool or even the leisure services department is operated inefficiently; the reduction in the quality of service is due to resource constraints, since those local authorities were 'charge-capped'. Many organizations in all sectors can justifiably say that the reason for poor service is resource constraints or external factors. However, this should not be the end of the story. Firstly, organizations should be aware of these constraints and take them into account when stating the level of service they can offer. Secondly, resource constraints are rarely the only reason for poor service. Organizations should not use them as an excuse for failing to look at themselves.

Next on the list of reasons for failure is being let down by suppliers. As we saw in chapter 1, delivering quality to the final customer depends on delivering quality to every customer in the customer–supplier chain. In order to do this TQM puts emphasis on developing new relationships with suppliers. Traditionally, relationships between customers and suppliers has been somewhat adversarial. This has been encouraged by having a number of suppliers who compete against each other, usually on the basis of price. TQM suggests a different way of doing things. First, a lot of effort should be put into specifying exactly what you expect of your supplier. There should then be a period of negotiation with the supplier, ending with a very clear agreement about what the supplier will be providing, when and how. This relationship should be a collaborative and long-term one. Although the relationship is collaborative it does not mean it is a soft one. Nissan cars carries out very little inspection of car components provided by its suppliers; it expects them all to be of high quality. If, however, there are warranty claims attributable to a supplier, Nissan expects the entire cost to be borne by the supplier.

One aspect of the new relationship between customers and suppliers is the notion of 'just in time'. This means that any items needed by a customer are delivered not well in advance, but just before the customer needs them. The dangers of this method are obvious: if the item is even slightly late the customer is disappointed; if the item is incorrect there is no time to check it, let alone replace it before use; the consequences of error are very great. Balanced against this is one huge advantage: there is an enormous cost saving because money is not tied up in stock or being spent on storage facilities. At one time, every Sainsbury's store used to have a very large stockroom. Large quantities of every item were kept, so that if a shop assistant noticed that an item in the shop had run out, she could go to the stockroom and find a replacement. This system had a number of disadvantages. First, shop assistants didn't always notice when the shelves in the shop became empty, and so some items were unavailable to customers. Second, if the item had run out in the stockroom, it often took weeks for a replacement to come from the suppliers. Third, it was very expensive having so much stock sitting in the stockroom. Sainsbury's now use a new system. As each item is passed over the checkout, a computer records the items used in that store. This is passed back to a central computer which orders the next day's supplies. These arrive just in time to replace the missing items on the shelves. Not only does this ensure that the shelves are never empty, it saves money.

The third reason for failing to deliver is internal inefficiency. While it may be tempting for managers simply to blame staff for being inefficient, lazy or demotivated, they are misleading themselves if they do so. The main causes of internal inefficiencies are managers who fail to put the correct systems in place.

Dorothy recently retired from her post as one of the assistant librarians at the central library. Although the head librarian had known for some time that she was going to retire, he had assumed that personnel would recruit a replacement as a matter of course. When he realized that this was not the case, there was a mad panic to begin the process of recruiting a replacement. The head librarian was much too busy to take an active part in the recruitment process, so personnel obligingly put an advertisement in the local paper and sent potential applicants a copy of Dorothy's old job description. When the interviews took place the head librarian did sit in on them; but as he hadn't had time to prepare, his judgement was based more on intuition than on any objective criteria. The personnel officer, who was the other person on the interview panel, had prepared thoroughly, but felt she should defer to the head librarian's views because after all he would have to work with whoever was appointed. As a result, the person given the job was rather like Dorothy in temperament, but didn't really have the relevant skills.

Apart from his failure to liaise properly with personnel, the head librarian had already made two mistakes. First, he had not taken a good look at what the requirements of the job were; the new person was being recruited to a job description which may have described Dorothy's job ten years ago but which certainly didn't accurately reflect what was required of that role now. Second, he effectively abdicated his responsibility for the interview process. If the wrong person is appointed to any job it is a disaster not only for the organization but also for that individual; no one likes to do tasks for which they lack the skills and experience. By relying only on his intuition the head librarian had missed the best person for the job.

Organizations which are committed to TQM put a huge effort into recruitment. Hewlett-Packard, the American electronics company gives job candidates ten or more interviews before making a job offer. Not only does this signal clearly to candidates that the company thinks people are important, it also enables managers to probe for the skills and qualities which are really necessary for the job – flexibility, creativity and ability to work as part of a team – qualities which are difficult to assess in one or two short interviews. Moreover, interviews at Hewlett-Packard are conducted not by personnel specialists but by managers. In this way managers take full responsibility for recruitment decisions. The role of the personnel recruitment service is then to train managers in interviewing techniques.

Dorothy was replaced by Cathy, and on her first day of work the head librarian was unfortunately on holiday. Although the librarians did their best to make Cathy welcome, none of them knew exactly what the head librarian had in mind for her. To some extent, Cathy's first week was spent passing time waiting for the head librarian to return. When he did, there was two weeks' backlog waiting on his desk, and he was able to give Cathy very little of his time. She picked up the job as best she could. This was the head librarian's third mistake: he continually failed to make it clear to Cathy what her role required of her. If there was a long queue of people waiting to get their books stamped she would go and help, only to be criticized later by the deputy head librarian for failing to catalogue her quota of books for the day. Eventually Cathy learned that her best strategy was to keep well out of the way and always look busy. Quality organizations have systems in place to make sure that everyone knows what is expected of them. This begins with a thorough induction programme for new staff and continues with regular one-to-one meetings between each member of staff and his or her manager. These sessions will be part information exchange, part problem solving (removing the barriers to good work), and part coaching, helping the staff member to develop new skills, knowledge and attitudes to do their job more effectively.

After Cathy had been in post a year, the head librarian was reminded by personnel that he had to conduct an annual appraisal. This was intended partly to give Cathy some feedback on her performance, and partly to make a decision on the size of her annual pay increment. As part of its policy to develop a more entrepreneurial and responsive style, the council as a whole had implemented a system of performance-related pay. This was the fourth mistake the head librarian was involved in. In principle an annual appraisal is a good idea, providing it is not a one-off but builds on regular feedback sessions throughout the year. Performance-related pay is not necessarily a bad idea but it must be fair and reward the right things. At the appraisal meeting the head librarian had to grade the new assistant librarian on a scale from 1 (outstanding) to 5 (grim). As he really hadn't much information to go on, and as most of Cathy's colleagues seemed to find her a pleasant member of the team, he graded her a 3 (acceptable). This entitled Cathy to a modest pay increase for the following year. This judgement was certainly not fair – had she been given proper support and training her performance could well have been outstanding – but neither was it rewarding the right things. Cathy could well have pointed out to the head librarian that the pressure on her to catalogue books meant that customers were having to queue too long; and perhaps suggested to him that the whole system of allocating job roles needed re-examining. She didn't do this because she knew that the head librarian didn't like change, and she was worried that if she made too much of a fuss she might be marked down to a 4 or even a 5. The pay system was rewarding compliance rather than service to customers.

Performance-related pay schemes are extremely difficult to implement in a fair way; but if an organization must have performance-related pay then it must reward the right things. Piecework systems are unacceptable because they reward quantity, not quality. Systems of performance-related pay which reward individual performance may operate against good team-work. Quality organizations should reward performance which contributes to long-term customer satisfaction. One way of doing this is to relate pay to the performance of the organization as a whole, rather than to the performance of individuals. Many commercial organizations do this through employee share-ownership schemes. Staff hold shares in the company, and benefit financially from dividend payments when the company is being successful. An alternative form of performance-related pay has recently been pioneered by one of the newly privatized water companies: employee pay is related to the quality of the water supplied. In this way the salary system is rewarding one of the most important components of customer satisfaction.

6 What can be done?

The task facing managers is easy to describe and difficult to do; it is to change the culture of the organization so that meeting customer needs genuinely becomes the main priority for everyone in the organization. Since people pay more attention to what is done than to what is said, managers should first begin by giving external customers more of their own attention. In many organizations, managers are protected from external customers by staff, who are often subtly and not so subtly encouraged to tell the manager what he or she would like to hear rather than the truth. Managers should make regular opportunities to have direct contact with staff. As part of the process of setting standards for the housing department, the director spent a day working on the enquiry desk of a housing aid centre, and a day answering phone calls from tenants in the maintenance and repair section. If the head librarian had spent more time stamping books and heard the muttered complaints of customers waiting in the queue, his attitude to staff management might have changed. All staff in an organization, whatever their role, should spend some time, even if it is just a day a year, in direct contact with external customers. Organizations should also have formal systems for finding out what customers want: focus groups, customer surveys, suggestion boxes. Domino's Pizza is a highly successful fast food chain in the USA. Each year they pay 10,000 mystery customers $60 each to buy a dozen pizzas each at various locations throughout the country, to evaluate the quality of the taste and service. Their comments are fed directly back to the managers of the restaurants concerned. The most important item on the agenda of any Domino's senior management meeting is the extent to which customer needs are being met.

If external customers are to feel satisfied with the service they receive, then the staff who deal directly with external customers must be skilled, confident and secure in their role. Yet in many organizations 'front line' staff are the most undervalued. They often receive the lowest pay and the least recognition. This must change; such staff should be given equal recognition to other employees. It is unfortunately commonplace in many British organizations for staff to say 'I know I'm doing OK if no one tells me off'. Staff should know they are doing well because they receive plenty of positive feedback. This can be provided not only from formal systems such as one-to-one meetings with a manager, but also quite informally.

Above all, organizations need to remove some of the bureaucracy which prevents staff from delivering good service to customers. Organizations which are serious about quality often find that they need to remove some of the layers of management. It is depressing for front line staff to feel that their efforts are effectively supporting layer upon layer of management, all of whom earn more than they do. No organization, however large, need have more than five layers between front line staff and chief executive. Reducing the number of management layers has a number of beneficial effects: it affirms the value of the people who 'do' as opposed to those who 'co-ordinate'; it also encourages managers to act less as overseers and controllers and more as coaches and enablers. With fewer layers of management, each manager inevitably becomes responsible for more staff, and is therefore obliged to give each individual more freedom and responsibility.

As managers spend less time overseeing and controlling work, so they have more time to improve organizational systems and procedures. They should be looking for opportunities to identify and eliminate both waste and wasted effort. In particular, they should aim to eliminate the need for systems of checking and remedying mistakes. This can be done by creating systems which are 'foolproof' – for example, designing machine parts so that it is impossible to put them together incorrectly – and by creating a climate where everyone believes in doing things right first time. To give a simple example of this, a manager could refuse to read her secretary's typing before signing it. By refusing to check someone else's work, the manager is encouraging the secretary to take full responsibility to get it right first time.

Organizations must set standards for the level of service which they will deliver to customers, standards which are continually improved upon. To what extent do standards imply standardization? At Domino's Pizza, for example, there are standardized procedures for preparing, cooking, serving and delivering pizza, which ensure consistency throughout the United States. Whether you order a Domino's pizza in New York, San Francisco or New Orleans it will taste the same and be delivered to your door in less than thirty minutes; if it is thirty-one minutes you pay nothing. Can such standards and procedures be used in situations where it is vital to treat people as individuals, such as social services or hospitals? Even in these settings, standards and procedures are helpful. When an ambulance crew arrives at the scene of a road traffic accident, the crew members do not rely entirely on their individual judgement as to who should be treated first and how; there are a set of procedures, which paramedics call protocols, which inform and guide their judgement. Within these protocols there is scope for individual discretion, just as there is at Domino's, where an employee would be rewarded for giving an extra portion of tomato ketchup to a customer whom she knew had a particular liking for it. Too many procedures and standards are as unhelpful as too few; a balance must be struck between standardized procedures and individual judgement. Indeed it is the role of managers to enable staff to use their judgement most appropriately.

3 The Tools of TQM

TQM often seems to be outrageously simple: find out what the customer wants and deliver it. As we have seen in the last chapter, this basic philosophy can be broken down into six questions, which though often difficult to answer help an organization move towards providing quality. Knowing the right questions to ask is very important, but only half the story; asking them of the right people, in the right way, in the right place, and at the right time, is much more difficult. Fortunately TQM offers a number of tools and techniques to do this, and they are examined in this chapter.

Organizing for quality

Quality doesn't happen by accident – it must be carefully planned and implemented. For this reason any organization which wishes to improve its quality should begin with a small group of people who are responsible for the process as a whole. This group is often called a quality council. The purpose of the group is not to answer the six questions, but to ensure that the questions are asked and answered by the right people. In other words it is in charge of the strategy for implementing TQM in the organization.

   Who should be on the quality council? Certainly the chief executive or equivalent. If TQM is to succeed it must not only have the support of the most senior member of staff, it must be seen to have this support. The council should also contain the other senior managers or directors of the organization, for similar reasons. Indeed, in many organizations the quality council is simply the senior management team operating under a different name. It is important that the work on quality is seen to be led and supported by a team, not just by one individual. Apart from anything else, TQM itself stresses the importance of good teamwork. It would be hypocritical to espouse an organizational philosophy which values teamwork and then impose it auto-cratically. Such a gap between what is said and what is done can cause great harm to an organization. Some organizations also appoint specialist quality managers. There is some danger in this: line managers may feel that quality can be left to the specialists, and that it is therefore no concern of theirs. However, there is a case for large organizations at least to have an in-house expert, especially in some of the more technical aspects of quality such as BS 5750.

One of the first tasks for the quality council is to draw up a quality policy. This policy will combine a statement of values – to the effect that the organization is committed to meeting the needs of its external customers – with some indication of the methods which will be used to achieve this end. This might include reference to customer–supplier chains, external suppliers, just-in-time techniques, the place of formal documentation, and so on. The purpose of this document is two-fold: it both provides a framework for developing a quality strategy, and the very process of drafting it will ensure that the members of the quality council understand the concepts for themselves. This quality policy should not be confused with the organization's business plan. The business plan is a statement of overall organizational objectives, and should clarify, for example, who the customers are. The quality policy contributes to the business plan by setting out some of the ways in which customer needs can be met.

Quality policies will vary in format from organization to organization; some will consist of a very brief outline of principles, others contain a great deal of detail. Here is a fairly typical example of a quality policy for a small service company.

Total Quality will be achieved by:

1. Creating an organizational climate which values honesty, integrity, innovation and equality of oppor-tunity.
2. The development and maintenance of excellent standards of communication across the company.
3. Continuous monitoring of the expectations of our external customers in respect of reliability, trustworthi-ness, expertise.

4. Ensuring that all staff treat internal customers with as much care and consideration as they would external customers.
5. Ensuring that all staff receive adequate training both in the skills relevant to their job role and in the principles of total quality.
6. Adopting a philosophy of continuous improvement in all work activities.

Having drawn up a quality policy, the quality council should prepare a strategy for implementing it. Various strategies are possible. Some organizations like to launch their quality initiative with a great deal of razzmatazz with posters, T-shirts, large meetings and public statements that from now on 'quality is the number one priority'. Other organizations prefer a much quieter approach, perhaps trying out some of the techniques in one part of the organization and then gradually extending it to others. Whatever strategy is used (and as we shall see later there are many possibilities), it is essential that it is well led, and that is the job of the quality council.

The quality council should also examine the costs of quality at an early stage in the implementation process. Putting TQM into place requires time and money and it would be irresponsible of any organization – whether in the private, public or social welfare sector – to embark on TQM without having done some kind of cost–benefit analysis: can the costs of TQM be justified in terms of the benefits to the organization?

The first step in the cost–benefit analysis is to work out how much the organization is currently spending on quality, or, to put it another way, how much it is currently spending on dealing with failures. There are three components to this. First, how much is currently being spent on work which is wasted, scrapped or has to be redone? This is the cost of internal failure. In an office it may be stationery which is ordered but never used; in a shop goods which are taken from the shelves because they are beyond their sell-by date; in a hospital beds which are not in use because there are not enough nurses to look after the patients who would occupy them. Some of this may be the result of bad planning, some the result of 'baker's dozen' philosophy. It is said that bakers who received an order for a dozen cakes used to send thirteen, in case one was spoilt. People in organizations often order more than they really need – whether it is office equipment, or stationery or raw materials – 'just in case'. In these examples the costs are easy to calculate because the waste is very visible; in other situations it is more difficult to identify and measure. Any wages for staff time spent on unnecessary work – that is, work which does not contribute to meeting customer needs – should be included in this category. I once worked on the night shift at an ice cream factory. We began work at 10 p.m. loading ice cream from a refrigerated warehouse into vans. We were usually finished by about 2 a.m. so we made ourselves as comfortable as we could in the (non-refrigerated!) storeroom where the ice cream cones were kept, and slept until the end of our shift at 6 a.m. In this case 50 per cent of the salary bill could be attributed to internal failure. Of course the net effect would have been the same if we had worked for fifteen minutes and been idle for fifteen minutes, a situation many workers find themselves in.

Next in the cost–benefit analysis is the cost of external failure. How much does it cost to remedy the poor products or services which do reach external customers? Under this heading should go the costs of dealing with customer complaints, handling returned goods and repairs, and warranty claims for failed products or services. In relation to its population, the United States spends more than twice as much on health care as the UK. Although this is partly due to the higher salaries paid to doctors, a large element of this difference may be attributed to the very high costs of insurance against being sued for malpractice. This cost of external failure is estimated to account for a fifth of the total expenditure on health care in the USA.

Then there are appraisal costs: how much time and money is spent on inspection and checking? This includes not only the cost of checking whether deliveries from external suppliers are up to scratch (and quality control checks on anything for external customers), but also the costs of internal checking and verification.

While it is often difficult to obtain a really accurate figure for the costs of internal failure, external failure and appraisal, it is important to have some idea. It is common for organizations to discover that something between a quarter and a third of all expenditure goes into these three areas. Instead, resources should be put into preventing waste and failure. As more resources are put into TQM and other systems for preventing failure – better staff training, better maintenance of machinery – the costs of failure and appraisal will fall, and the overall level of quality will go up. Establishing this case is what a cost–benefit analysis is all about.

Teamwork

TQM puts an enormous emphasis on teamwork, and there are a number of reasons for this. First, there is a lot of evidence to show that a well-organized team can perform much better than a collection of individuals. This phenomenon is known as synergy – the whole is greater than the sum of the parts. Synergy is well illustrated in an exercise which is commonly used as part of a TQM training programme. Course participants are asked to imagine that they are temporarily stranded on the moon. Each participant is asked to rank in terms of usefulness a list of fifteen items which might help them to survive: water, parachute silk, oxygen tanks, rope and so on. Once individuals have made their rankings, groups of five or six participants are asked to undertake the same task. At the end of the exercise both individual and group rankings are compared with the 'correct answer' as provided by NASA. Almost without exception, the group ranking scores more highly than the average of the individual rankings, and in a majority of cases the group ranking score is higher than the highest individual ranking.

Teamwork also has the advantage that people usually have more commitment to a decision they were involved in making than to a decision taken by someone else. During Margaret Thatcher's term of office as Prime Minister, two major pieces of legislation became law, the Community Charge (or Poll Tax) and the Children Act. Both made radical changes to existing law, in the way local taxes were raised on the one hand, and in the way children are treated in a wide variety of situations on the other. Both were initially controversial and unpopular pieces of legisla-tion. The Community Charge was subject to fairly little consultation, and by and large the results of consultation were ignored. In contrast, the Children Act was subject to very wide consultation indeed, and the original proposals were very considerably modified as a result. Several years later the Community Charge has now been completely abandoned in favour of the Council Tax, whereas the Children Act is firmly in place and generally supported by the local authorities and social welfare agencies which have the task of implementing it. The moral for organizations is clear: it may be time consuming to involve people in consultation and teamwork, but it pays off in long-term results.

Unfortunately, there is a potential negative side to creating strong and effective teams. There is evidence to show that the better the co-operation within each team, the more the antagonism and rivalry between teams. This phenomenon is illustrated by a famous experiment carried out in 1949. Sherif and Sherif selected a sample of 24 boys for a summer camp in Connecticut, USA. The boys were selected to be as nearly similar in age, social origin, education and a number of other factors. After the first few days of the camp in which the boys were left to sort themselves out spontaneously, they were divided into two new groups which deliberately cut across the emerging friendships. After a further five days, the boys were asked to say who they liked best out of the 24 boys. The original patterns of friendship were now completely reversed. Moreover, what had started as friendly rivalry between the two groups degenerated into an outright war. By the end of the camp the two groups were throwing food and crockery at each other during mealtimes.

Rivalry between teams and departments is extremely common in most organizations. Indeed it is rare to find a manufacturing company where there is harmony between marketing and production, or a charity where there is no tension between the fundraisers and the operational departments. From the TQM point of view, <u>effective teamwork means good co-operation between teams, as well as within them.</u> Good teamwork is rare in organizations partly because the skills needed to work effectively in a team are very great. As well as creating opportunities for people to work in teams TQM also pays attention to training them in the skills required. It provides three frameworks for developing good teamwork: quality circles, departmental purpose audits, and quality improvement teams. These provide opportunities to improve teamwork within work groups, within departments, and across departments.

Quality circles

For many people, quality circles are almost synonymous with TQM, and yet they are probably one of the least understood and least successful TQM techniques, in the UK at least. A quality circle consists of a small group of workers who normally work together on similar or identical tasks. They meet regularly, during work time but on a voluntary basis. The idea is to identify problems, analyse them and find solutions. In some cases these solutions can be implemented immediately by the workers themselves, in other cases they are presented to management for their approval. Quality circles are led by the regular team leader.

In principle quality circles sound a great ideal, harnessing the expertise and ingenuity of the workforce themselves to improve quality and productivity. When they do work they achieve all this and a real sense of commitment to the task. If quality circles are to be successful, a number of preconditions must be met. Attendance must be genuinely voluntary. This is usually not too much of a problem, since they take place in work time and most people welcome the chance to stop doing their regular job for a while and talk about it instead. All members of the quality circle must do similar work. For many organizations who like the sound of TQM this is more of an obstacle. While it may be common in very large manufacturing organizations for there to be groups of people who do the same job together, in other settings there tends to be a much higher degree of job specialization; ten people may work together in the personnel department but they all have different roles – salaries, employees relations, recruitment and so on. For this reason alone quality circles may be inappropriate for some organizations.

Quality circles must have the full support of management. This can be very problematic. It often happens that one group of managers is very enthusiastic to set up quality circles to find another group trying to disband them. Some managers view quality circles as giving staff time off to gripe about the company. Alternatively, managers may express a verbal commitment to quality circles but be unwilling to provide the necessary training. Quality circles call for a very high level of skills: the team leader must be able to run meetings; team members need the skills of collaborative problem solving. Finally, quality circles need the support of any relevant unions. The relationship between TQM and unions has been a somewhat uneasy one. On the one hand the ethos of teamwork and empowerment is entirely consistent with the notion of industrial democracy which unions support. On the other hand, many unions see TQM as just another form of managerial control, and these fears are increased by companies like Nissan and IBM which do not recognize unions for the purposes of negotiations.

Quality circles have not been a great success in the UK. Even companies like IBM and Rover who claim great success for other TQM activities, have largely abandoned quality circles. A fairly typical British experience of quality circles is demonstrated by the story of a West Midlands engineering firm. In the late seventies both the technical manager and the personnel manager had quite independently become interested in quality circles. When they learnt of their mutual interest they decided to set about implementing them. Initially they set up a briefing meeting for managers and supervisors in the production department, where quality circles were to be first introduced. Representatives from the two main unions were invited to this meeting, but they didn't attend. Everyone seemed very interested in the concept, so it was agreed to set up six quality circles in various parts of the factory. Although the technical manager wasn't that keen, the personnel manager persuaded him that some training was required first. She led a one-day session in the skills of problem solving and leading meetings for the supervisors who would lead the quality circles and for their managers.

The six quality circles began to meet immediately the training was finished. One of the groups achieved an immediate and spectacular success: by finding a new way of setting up the machines, they were able to reduce the defect rate from 30 per cent to less than 3 per cent, saving the company something like £5,000 a year. One of the other groups seemed to be going reasonably well, but the other four less so. Their meetings tended to degenerate into general moaning rather than solving specific problems. The technical manager and the personnel manager had some urgent meetings about this. The quality circles had now been running for almost three months and there was pressure on them to show some more successes. They agreed that it would give the quality circles more focus if the departmental managers gave them some specific problems to solve. This was done and it made matters worse; quality circles rely on commitment of the members, and this is reduced if members are not identifying problems for themselves. To make matters even worse, one of the unions began complaining that the workers were being blamed for not solving problems that the management should have sorted out in the first place. Shortly after this there was a sharp downturn in demand for the firm's products which resulted in 200 of the firm's 900 staff being laid off. Senior managers were keen to see all the remaining staff at their machines for the whole of every shift. Morale was generally very low and there was little enthusiasm for collaborative problem solving. The quality circles were all abandoned.

With hindsight the personnel and technical managers saw that they had made a number of errors: they hadn't secured the wholehearted support of all senior managers for the scheme; they should have made more efforts to find out why the unions hadn't attended the initial meeting; and they hadn't provided enough training either for themselves or for the supervisors to make sure everyone fully understood the concept.

There is however a happy ending to this story. The success of the quality circle in identifying better ways of setting up machines convinced a number of senior managers that there were considerable savings to be made not just in shedding staff but by improving systems and procedures. Several years after the quality circles episode, the production director instituted a programme of developing procedures and standards for setting up and operating the machines. This led to a full quality assurance initiative, and eventually to the company being awarded the British Standard for quality assurance, BS 5750.

Departmental purpose audits

A departmental purpose audit (DPA) is similar to a quality circle in that it is a technique for improving quality through teamwork. It differs from a quality circle in that the team members, although they work in the same department, have different job roles. It is led by the departmental head, who has a clear personal incentive to improve the performance of his or her department. This is how it works.

Step one
- Form a DPA group. This should contain the department head and representatives from each of the main activities within the department, though not necessarily the most senior people. Ideally there should be around six people in the group.
- List all the tasks of the department.
- Prioritize the most important five tasks.
- Define the role of the departmental head.
- Review the five main tasks of the department and identify customers and suppliers.

Step two
- Meet with customers and suppliers to agree what they expect and can offer.

Step three
- DPA group meets to review results and prioritize areas for improvement.
- Brainstorm possible improvements.
- Prioritize improvements.
- Implement improvement plan.

Like quality circles, DPAs are led by the work group leader, in this case the departmental manager, and their success depends largely on the skills of this person. It is vital for the departmental head to be open minded, to encourage questioning and creativity, and to feel confident in his or her own abilities as a team leader; after all, the departmental head's role will be discussed explicitly as part of the DPA.

Kirit Modi is a newly appointed administration director for a national charity. His department is responsible for all the behind the scenes activities which makes such an organization run smoothly. When he was appointed he decided to organize a departmental purpose audit. He first brought together the supervisors of the main sections within the administration department: office services, the print room, caretaking, the staff canteen. Together they listed the main functions of the department and identified customers and suppliers. Although everyone at the meeting thought this was a good idea, there was some anxiety. Some of the supervisors thought they might be blamed for things that were out of their control; the canteen supervisor, for example, admitted that the quality of the food was not good but put this down to poor equipment and a limited budget. Nevertheless each section head agreed to meet with representatives of their customers to find out how well their needs were being met. What helped the process immensely was the fact that Kirit encouraged open discussion about his own role. It became clear that all of the supervisors had felt very unsupported by Kirit's predecessor, and were able to make some specific requests for how they would like Kirit to support them in the future.

After the meetings with customers had taken place, the DPA group met again. The feedback from customers had been mixed: most people had been very appreciative of the post room's service, and most were very critical of the canteen and the print room. Kirit was keen to involve everyone in finding solutions to problems in all areas of the administration department, so he set up a set of meetings to problem solve on one area at a time. The first of these meetings focused on the canteen. Once again, the canteen supervisor was initially very anxious, but became more confident when it became clear that Kirit was more interested in finding ways forward than in attributing blame. A list of over thirty possible improvements to the canteen was brainstormed. This list was then discussed and four specific actions were agreed on. These were:

1. Conduct further full-scale customer survey to gain more information on what customers want.
2. Take up an offer of help from a commercial catering company to redesign the kitchens and install new equipment.

3. Provide training for the canteen supervisor.
4. Renegotiate contract with three main suppliers to the kitchen.

As these actions were set in train for the canteen, further meetings were arranged to review the other priority areas, beginning with the print room. The entire process lasted nearly a year, and by the end of it the quality of service had increased enormously. Not only did the DPA have direct results in terms of the quality of service, but it also developed a strong sense of teamwork between the people working in the various sections of the department.

Quality improvement team

We have already encountered this technique in chapter 1. It consists of people from different departments working together on a particular topic. Unlike quality circles and DPAs it has a limited life – when that particular problem is resolved it is disbanded. Members are chosen according to their appropriateness for the task in hand. They do not need to be of the same seniority in the organization, neither does the team leader need to be the most senior person in the group. However, the quality improvement team does need a sponsor, a senior person or group of people in the organization who have the authority to implement any changes suggested by the quality improvement team. However brilliant the suggestions made by the quality improvement team, the effort will have been wasted unless their ideas are actually put into practice. This is unlikely to happen unless there is support from senior management, the people with the authority to implement changes.

Training

If people are to do things better, they must not only want to do things differently, they must have the skills and knowledge to do so. That is why training is central to any TQM initiative. In some organizations training is for managers only, often in the form of very expensive management development courses. In other organizations managers feel themselves to be somehow above training, which is considered relevant only to the workers. Both these attitudes are wrong – training is for everybody.

Since the wrong kind of training is worse than no training at all, any training programme must be based on a sound analysis of training needs. These fall broadly into three categories. First, there are training needs relevant to the organization as a whole. At some stage in the implementation of TQM it is likely that everyone will need to be informed about the broad principles of quality improvement: customer–supplier chains, understanding customer needs, eliminating waste. Often this kind of training is cascaded down an organization; first the directors are trained, then the senior managers, then the middle managers, supervisors and staff. The initial training of directors and senior managers is usually by consultants or other experts, but often internal trainers deliver the later courses. A second set of training needs relates to specific departments or projects. If a department wants to carry out a departmental purpose audit, or to set up a quality improvement team, then training will be required to develop these skills. An effective quality improvement team facilitator should be able to use fishbone charts and Pareto analysis to analyse problems, lead a collaborative problem-solving session in which people stick to the task and value each other's opinion, and chair meetings which finish on time. This is a lot to ask of anyone without training. Finally, individuals have training needs relating to their own job. Many organizations have some system of appraisal or staff development interviews to ensure that individual training needs are identified. Those that do not will need to set one up before implementing TQM.

Once needs have been identified they can be met. In some cases this will mean training, either on an in-house course or by sending people to an external course. In other cases some non-course based forms of training will be more appropriate. Possibilities include on-the-job instruction, secondments, job rotation, computer-based training, coaching and mentoring. Increasingly, organizations are relying less on specialists to deliver training, and expecting managers to act as coach, tutor and mentor. A survey recently compared the approaches to management training in successful Japanese companies and their

British counterparts. All the Japanese companies in the survey had well established TQM programmes. Only half of the British companies were initiating some kind of quality programme. At first the results were surprising: Japanese managers spent significantly less time on management courses than British managers. However, the Japanese managers spent nearly three times as much time on development activities such as job rotation, coaching and self-development, than the British. In a way this is common sense. If you attend a course on TQM you may return full of enthusiasm. You then discover that the course wasn't quite as relevant to your department as you'd thought, and that your boss isn't going to give you much support in implementing the ideas from the course because she doesn't fully understand them herself. By way of contrast, if your understanding of TQM had come from being coached by your boss, not only would your own understanding be that much deeper because it would be rooted in the context of your own job, but you could be reasonably confident that your boss would support any TQM initiatives you wished to make.

The survey showed some other marked differences between the Japanese and British companies. British managers tended to say that 'either you've got it or you haven't' in relation to management, whereas Japanese managers believed that management skills could be learnt by virtually everyone. 15 per cent of the British felt that role models or mentors had been important in their development; for the Japanese it was 70 per cent. Whereas some of the British managers felt they had been lucky to have been given challenging positions at an early age, such assignments were routine in Japan. The term 'management development' while common in Britain, was almost unheard of in Japanese companies, who spoke of the need to increase the capability of everyone in their job role; and in general development activities in the Japanese companies were more closely linked to the demands of the job.

While training is a very important component of TQM, it cannot solve every problem. If someone comes to repair my washing machine, and she has not been supplied with the correct tools of the job, no amount of training will enable her to provide me with a quality service. If her employers are in the midst of a major programme of redundancies, she may not be motivated to do a good job, and no amount of training will change her attitude. The real blocks to quality in organizations often revolve around resources, job design and attitudes, and these must be resolved first before training can usefully be offered.

Tools for measuring and recording

Many approaches to organizational effectiveness stress the importance of achieving the commitment of the workforce. TQM is no exception to this; it stresses the necessity of achieving a complete culture change, old attitudes being washed away by new thinking based on customer satisfaction, eliminating waste and continuous improvement. The benefits come from releasing the talents, energy and commitment of everyone in the organization. However, there is another side of TQM which is concerned with measurement, analysis and systematic approaches to problem solving. As we have already seen in chapter 2, a warm smile and an intuitive feel for what customers want is not enough; quality must be measured and causes of failure rigorously analysed. We have already met one way of measuring quality, by use of performance indicators. TQM makes use of a number of other tools and techniques for measuring and recording quality. Some of these techniques are applicable only to certain organizations where it is vital to measure very large amounts of complex numerical data (industrial chemicals, for example). Many of the tools, however, can be useful in almost any organization, and in this section I have chosen the seven most popular TQM tools. They are not unique to TQM, but they are an integral part of it. They are:

- fishbone charts and Pareto analysis for analysing problems;
- brainstorming to devise solutions;
- Gantt charts and flowcharts to plan and implement solutions;
- tally charts and histograms to monitor progress.

Each of these techniques is now explored in turn. Some people find this talk of measurement and analysis rather tedious; on many TQM training courses it is the idea which is often resisted the most. However, when people do see its relevance they often report that it has been one of the most useful parts of the course. So if you are tempted to skip this section, at least give it a try. This 'scientific' side of TQM is just as important as the 'human relations' side. Both are needed if TQM is to be effectively implemented in any organization.

Fishbone charts

In order to remedy any organizational problem it is important to look beyond the symptoms of the problem to the root causes. All too often, however, this is not done; there is pressure on managers to go for a 'quick fix' and to respond to the symptoms, not to treat the root causes. TQM offers a number of techniques for getting to the roots of a problem, and the most popular of these is called the fishbone chart. In chapter 1 the confectionery company was having trouble with the wrappers on its chocolate bars. A number of reasons for this immediately spring to mind: perhaps the printing machine was at fault; perhaps it was being operated incorrectly; perhaps it was being supplied with the wrong paper or ink. This initial analysis gives us the first stage of the fishbone chart.

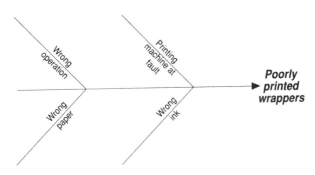

Fig. 5

This initial analysis has really just revealed the symptoms of the problem. In order to get to the root causes each of the possible reasons is explored further. If the machine was at fault had it been maintained correctly? If not had the maintenance programme been reduced to save costs or had the maintenance engineer not been trained properly? By exploring each of the causes as much as possible the final fishbone chart is constructed.

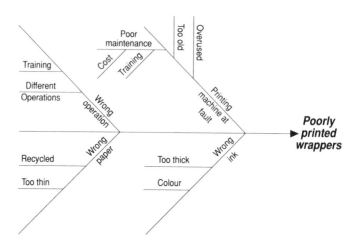

Fig. 6

You can see why it is called a fishbone chart. It is also sometimes referred to as an Ishikawa diagram, after its originator. In many cases a thorough analysis of the problem will point clearly to the remedy required. In the case of the confectionery firm the problem had actually been caused by a change of paper for the labels. The printer did not know what adjustments were needed to the machine to print recycled paper which was rather more absorbent than the old kind. A telephone call to the suppliers of the printing machine resolved the difficulty once and for all.

Pareto analysis

In the example above, the poor quality of the wrappers was attributable to a relatively small number of causes. In other situations however problems have multiple causes; there may be literally hundreds of reasons why customers complain about a particular service. Pareto analysis offers a simple but powerful tool for separating the significant items in a mass of data. Vilfredo Pareto was an Italian economist who observed that 80 per cent of the wealth in his country was owned by 20 per cent of the people. He then noticed that in very many situations 80 per cent of the outcomes seemed to be attributable to 20 per cent of the causes, and this observation is now known as the Pareto principle. So, for example, most charities receive around 80 per cent of their income from just 20 per cent of their donors. Many shops earn 80 per cent of their income from just 20 per cent of their product lines.

When Kirit Modi took over the administration department, his predecessor handed him a long list of complaints about the way the department had been run. At first this list was somewhat overwhelming. However, Kirit knew that if the Pareto principle applied in this case, a relatively small number of areas should be responsible for most of the complaints. He analysed the complaints into ten main categories as follows.

Poor food in canteen	38%
Poor service from print room	32%
General office cleaning	9%
Repairs service	6%
Stationery deliveries	3%
Internal phone directory	3%
Reception	3%
Security	2%
Internal post	1%
Other	3%

It was then clear that 20 per cent of the department's work – the canteen and print room – was responsible for, in this case, 70 per cent of the complaints. The canteen and print room would be priority areas for attention.

Although the Pareto principle does not apply exactly in all circumstances – in the example above there seemed to be a 20–70 rule at work rather than a 20–80 rule – it does seem to apply at least approximately in very many. A local authority finance department knew that they were receiving many invoices for payment which had been incorrectly prepared. At first sight there seemed to be such a huge range of errors that the effort of remedying them all was too great. The Pareto principle suggested that it was worth trying to see if a relatively small number of causes – perhaps around 20 per cent of possible input errors – could be causing most – around 80 per cent – of the output errors. A detailed analysis of the input errors showed this to be the case. Nearly 80 per cent of the errors were caused by data processing clerks coding invoices incorrectly. A small adjustment was made to the computer's accounting system which made the computer bleep if the coding was inconsistent with the originating department. As a result the overall error rate was drastically reduced.

Brainstorming

Analysing the reasons for problems is one thing; finding solutions is another. Brainstorming is a very common technique for reaching creative solutions to problems, and is also the most misunderstood. Brainstorming properly works like this. The problem to be addressed is written down and members of the brainstorming group are invited to suggest ideas, thoughts, inspirations and guesses towards solving it. The quantity of ideas is as important as the quality at this stage, and zany or offbeat suggestions are particularly welcome. Most importantly, every idea should be written down exactly as the speaker intends it. It is at this point that brainstorms often go wrong: all too often the group leader, or the person with the pen, changes what the speaker actually said, or even omits to record some suggestions. It is vital to write everything, pretty much verbatim, if the creativity is not to be lost. Once all the ideas have been recorded, the second stage can begin. Ideas are discussed, discarded and developed. Group members should aim to build on and develop each other's ideas, not advocating their own. Gradually the most promising ideas are opened up and unsuitable options left behind. By the end of this discussion a solution, or solutions, will have been identified for further investigation.

In the late sixties a group of people who worked for a major bank were discussing the problem of how to give customers greater access to banking facilities without having to pay staff overtime for extended opening hours. During the course of a brainstorm someone suggested knocking a hole in the wall of the bank so that customers could walk in and help themselves to money at any time. In the course of the discussion which followed, this idea was gradually refined into the idea of knocking a hole in the wall and putting a machine in there to serve customers. This was the first mention of the automatic teller machines which are so common in banks and building societies today.

Gantt charts

When people work together in a team, different team members usually have different tasks to do which take differing lengths of time. It is frustrating for one team member to have to wait while another finishes a task before she can continue with her job. There are various fairly complicated techniques for ensuring that this does not happen (including critical path analysis and flow line balancing). However one of the most useful and straightforward methods for planning and scheduling work is called a Gantt chart, and an example is shown in figure 7. It is named after the man who first developed it. This particular chart is for a small community association which is organizing an annual general meeting. The letter of invitation cannot be sent until it is typed; it

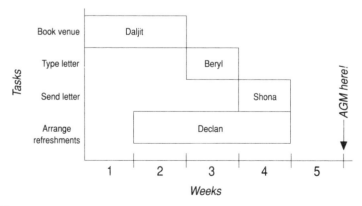

Fig. 7

cannot be typed before the venue is booked. On the other hand, arranging refreshments can be done at any time. The Gantt chart displays tasks, identifies who is responsible for what, and gives an idea of the overall timescale.

Flowcharts

Flowcharts are useful for planning new procedures. The example given shows the routine for accepting payment in a small grocery store (which doesn't accept Switch or credit cards). Flowcharts are also a very useful tool to clarify existing procedures and identify any areas of waste. In the example given below, is it really necessary for the supervisor to check £50 notes?

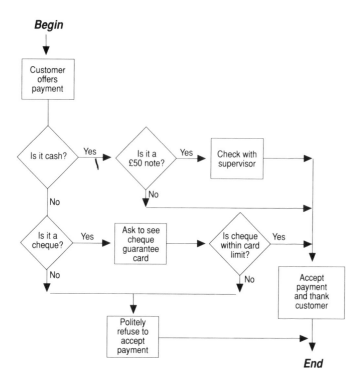

Fig. 8

Tally charts and histograms

The examples shown in figure 9 provide a visual reminder of quality for a group of people working in a stockroom. Their aim is to send out 90 per cent of orders within a day and the two charts record their success.

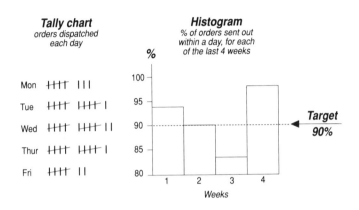

Fig. 9

BS 5750

The British Standards Institution (BSI) is an official body which sets nationally and internationally recognized standards for a whole range of products and services. Most of its standards refer to a particular product or service; so, for example, BS 7070 sets standards for the purity of unleaded petrol and BS 5423 is concerned with the construction of fire extinguishers. BS 5750 is unusual in that it applies not to the product or service itself, but to the process by which any product or service is provided. Compliance with BS 5750 involves an examination of every aspect of an organization's activities, from the way orders are taken through to the satisfactory completion of a delivery. BS 5750 is proof that the organization consistently delivers high quality services to its customers. It can be applied to any organization, irrespective of size, activity and whether it is a private, public or voluntary sector body.

BS 5750 was first developed over ten years ago, but has only become generally known in the last few years. In 1987 it was adopted by the International Standards Institution as ISO 9000. The process of obtaining BS 5750/ISO 9000 is known as *third party certification*. If your own organization sets its own quality standards it is first party certification, and if they are agreed by your customers this is second party certification. Third party certification involves a neutral outside body like the BSI.

As I mentioned in chapter 1, there are at least three broad approaches to quality. The Quality Control approach is based on last minute checking to remove any duds before the final customer receives them. The Quality Assurance approach involves a review of the whole process to find a way of delivering quality every time. When a satisfactory level has been achieved it is written up in a quality manual. In the TQM approach, the whole system is reviewed, but no level of quality is ever deemed satisfactory; the quest is for continuous improvement. BS 5750 sits firmly in the second camp; it is a quality assurance tool.

Once a company is registered as having achieved BS 5750, it is entitled to use the Registered Firm symbol (the BSI 'kitemark') on its letterheads and publicity material. This is in effect a statement issued by an independent third party that the organization operates in a manner that ensures its services consistently meet what it has promised to its customers. This is in itself a major promotional asset. Neither are the gains merely in the organization's image; in most cases BS 5750 does actually improve the quality of service provided. For example most organizations who achieve BS 5750 experience something like a 50 per cent drop in customer complaints and claims. This is particularly true for organizations which depend on working to accurate schedules and procedures. A family-owned firm of printers had a reputation for friendliness and flexibility but found it was losing business to a local rival who was able to guarantee delivery times for printed material. The family firm had a rather chaotic system for scheduling work based largely on dealing with whatever was at the top of the pile first. If a job had any unusual requirements – unusually coloured inks, for example –

production virtually ground to a halt while the head printer drove to the suppliers to pick up whatever was needed. The process of BS 5750 certification enabled the company to develop procedures which guaranteed delivery times for different kinds of job, delivery times which were substantially quicker than their nearest rivals. The firm's profitability more than doubled as a result.

BS 5750 can in some cases reduce the amount of bureaucracy in an organization. A local authority waste disposal department had nearly 2,000 pages of manuals and instructions for dealing with various types of hazardous waste. These manuals had simply grown as new legislation and new types of chemical waste had appeared. Inevitably the service was very slow; it sometimes took an officer the best part of a day just to identify how a particular chemical should be disposed of. The process of BS 5750 certification enabled these manuals to be rewritten in the form of a basic 40-page manual with references to a few other key documents. The department is now able to respond to over 95 per cent of requests for waste disposal in less than an hour.

Although there are many advantages to BS 5750 there are also a number of drawbacks. Since BS 5750 is essentially a quality assurance technique, it can prove a barrier to the continuous improvement which TQM advocates. BS 5750 effectively guarantees consistent delivery of a particular level of quality, a level of quality which may not be particularly high. I once had the opportunity to eat a truly dreadful meal in a hospital canteen, which proudly displayed its BS 5750 registration document. Later that day I met the canteen manager and pointed out the apparent inconsistency between the meal and the certificate. He agreed that the food was bad; but with BS 5750 it was at least consistently bad. I do not think he was joking.

Also on the debit side for BS 5750 is the fact that it sometimes seems to be a case of using a sledgehammer to crack a nut. Many small organizations – particularly sole traders in the private sector – really do not need a formally documented quality assurance procedure. The procedures are already operating very effectively out of the proprietor's head. If for example the Plumbers Federation made BS 5750 a condition of membership it would oblige many independent plumbers to spend large sums of money on a certification process which may not improve the quality of the service at all.

This brings us to the topic of contract compliance. Many organizations in the private, public and social welfare sectors are insisting that their suppliers are BS 5750 registered. This can be very positive. If, for example, a health authority is awarding a contract to private or voluntary agencies to run children's homes, it is important that the health authority should have some guarantee of the quality of provision. BS 5750 is one way of doing this. This is acceptable providing that not too much emphasis is put on BS 5750. As we have seen BS 5750 guarantees consistency more than it does quality. Moreover, there may be other excellent suppliers who have chosen not to register either on the grounds of time or cost (registration can take between six months and a year and cost upward of £10,000) or because they are genuinely committed to TQM and continuous improvement, not merely to Quality Assurance.

The procedure for obtaining BS 5750 works like this. You should first contact the British Standards Institution or one of the other dozen or so validating bodies. They will ask you to fill in a preliminary application form. They will then be able to advise you which part of BS 5750 is most relevant to your organization. BS 5750 part 1 is for organizations which tailor-make specific services for their customers, for example architects or management consultants. It is generally more difficult to achieve than BS 5750 part 2 which is for organizations who provide services to an established design, for example a chocolate factory. The next step is to draw up a quality manual for your organization. This should be a statement of what your organization does to deliver a quality service to customers; not what senior management would like to be done, nor what some management consultant thinks could be done, but what is actually done. This quality manual, which may be 30 plus pages long, has to cover certain areas specified by BS 5750. These include answers to the following questions:

- What are the organization's management structures?
- How are new products and services designed?
- What systems are used to select new suppliers, and to monitor the quality of existing ones?

- What work instructions are available to staff, and are they adhered to?
- Are there records of all quality assurance activities?
- What systems are in place for sampling and testing?
- What systems are in place for remedying any deviations from specified performance?
- What systems are in place for storage and handling of materials?
- Do all staff have accurate job descriptions?
- Are appropriate staff training programmes in place?

This quality manual should be sent to the validating body who will check to see that it covers the ground set out in BS 5750. They will then send a team of assessors to visit your organization to assess whether the quality manual actually describes what happens in your organization. At the end of this visit the assessors will tell you whether your organization can be awarded BS 5750, or whether there is further work to be done. Assuming you have been successful, you can expect to receive between two and four 'surveillance visits' each year. These are designed to ensure that you continue to work to BS 5750 standards. If the BSI officers notice any discrepancies, you are expected not only to remedy them, but to add a new section to the quality manual to ensure that these particular discrepancies never happen again. In extreme cases BS 5750 certification can be removed altogether.

This description of the BS 5750 certification process is considerably simplified; it is a very complex and time-consuming procedure. Despite this, more and more organizations are going down this route. BS 5750 registration is by far the fastest growing area of the BSI's activities.

4 Implementing TQM

Implementing TQM in any organization requires a huge amount of change. Old systems of control and checking must be removed and new systems put in their place: quality councils, quality improvement teams, departmental purpose audits. People must change: new attitudes are needed which stress the importance of meeting customer needs, and this includes the internal customer as well as the final, external customer; capabilities must increase, managers and staff must be able to do their jobs more skilfully; and above all behaviour must change.

There are two very common misperceptions of managing organizational change. The first of these is that managers are all-powerful when it comes to changing their organizations. This view is often promoted by management consultants and writers, who give the impression that by following certain steps, senior managers can be sure to transform their organizations. The second misperception takes the opposite point of view, that even senior managers are powerless to change their organizations. In my work as a management consultant, I am often struck by the fact that directors and chief executives, who may be drawing large salaries, see themselves as basically powerless to change the nature of the organization for which they are responsible. Instead they see the power as being vested with government, unions, local councillors or some other group.

The truth, of course, lies midway between the two. It is certainly not easy to bring about organizational change. Even very small organizations are highly complex entities, and change can never be brought about by a simple set of prescriptions. Outside factors do play an important part; as many small businesses have found to their cost during the recent recession, even the best run organization can be driven out of business by bad debts or high interest rates. Nevertheless managers – and staff – are not powerless. In equally difficult circumstances, some organizations thrive while others fall by the wayside, and the crucial difference is the quality of the people leading them. Managers do have power and how they use it makes a difference. In order to bring about organizational change there are three major factors to consider.

- Are people ready for change?
- What is the best strategy for change?
- What is the best leadership style?

We will consider these three questions before looking at some case studies of organizational change involving TQM.

Readiness to change

Most people don't like change imposed upon them. To take but one example, there was tremendous resistance to the introduction of a pound coin to replace the old pound note in England and Wales in the late 1980s. Now that most people are used to these coins, there would no doubt be huge resistance to the idea of returning to paper notes once again. In many situations, it is a case of 'better the devil you know than the one you don't'. Implementing TQM, however, involves a massive amount of personal and organizational change. In what circumstances are people likely to be ready for change? In this section we will explore <u>four factors</u> which predispose people to accepting change: the presence of an external threat; internal dissatisfaction; a vision of how things could be better; and a knowledge of the first practical steps.

There is nothing like an <u>external threat</u> to make people ready for change. Huge changes in British working life were accepted during the early 1940s, largely in response to the threat posed by the Second World War. For organizations today, the threats are likely to come from commercial competition, or government legislation, or both. The considerable changes in the UK motor industry over the last ten years or so are largely attributable to the threat of competition (from Japanese and European manufacturers) and government legislation (in respect of both privatization and trade unions).

Very often organizations have plenty of time to become aware of external pressures and respond to them, using TQM where appropriate. Small independent hardware shops had virtually the whole of the 1970s to become aware of the rise of the large discount DIY chains such as Texas and B&Q and to make an appropriate response, in some cases using the principles of TQM to identify and meet the needs of a particular niche of customers. Similarly, charitable organizations working with children have had a number of years' warning of the effects which the Children Act would have on their activities, before it was finally implemented in 1990. In this situation, changes based on TQM would have been appropriate. In other situations, external pressures take the form of a sudden crisis: an organization suddenly loses its biggest (and perhaps only) customer. In such a crisis situation, while the organization may be ready for TQM, this may not be the best response. TQM is not a quick fix; it almost always takes months, if not years to implement. In a crisis situation requiring very rapid action some other kind of measure – emergency cost-cutting for example – might be more appropriate. TQM can follow later. Ironically, had TQM been in place earlier, such a sudden crisis probably would not have occurred.

People will also change if they are dissatisfied with the existing situation within the organization. If staff are unhappy with working conditions, pay, job satisfaction, or the quality of service they are able to provide, then they will at least be open to the idea of doing things differently. The Zone Gallery in Newcastle is a photographic gallery with an excellent reputation amongst professional photographers and secure funding from its regional arts board. In that sense there are no external pressures to change. However the staff of the gallery are becoming increasingly dissatisfied that despite working very long hours only a comparatively small number of people are using the gallery. This sense of internal dissatisfaction has prompted them to undertake a major development programme for the gallery including opening a café and education project. Often it is external pressures which lead to internal dissatisfaction. In fact one of the most useful roles that managers and consultants can play at the beginning of the change management process is to *increase* the level of internal dissatisfaction by making staff aware of the external pressures facing the organization.

The third situation in which people will be ready for change is the presence of a sufficiently inspiring vision of how things could be. In 1964 a woman called Steve Shirley set up a small business called Freelance Programmers, to enable her to earn a living from writing computer programs at home. She also had a much bigger vision: to provide opportunities for other women who wished to develop and use computing skills but who were unwilling, or unable, to travel to a full-time office job. As a result of this vision she was able to transform Freelance Programmers into an organization (now called F International) with over 1,000 staff and a turnover of over £20m a year. Many organizations are initiated and transformed by such visions: Body Shop and the vision of environmentally friendly products; Save the Children and the vision to protect the rights of children and young people; even the Post Office and the vision to provide the best postal service in the world. If a vision is to create a readiness for change, it must be not only exciting and creative, it must also be specific, it must paint a clear picture of exactly how things would appear if the vision became reality. Steve Shirley's vision wasn't just a vague notion of more opportunities for women, it was a very specific image of women, based at home, working on computers and networking with each other.

Unless the vision is particularly inspiring, it usually isn't enough to create a readiness for change; a fourth factor is required and that is a knowledge of the first practical steps. It isn't necessary to map out the whole route from the present situation to the desired vision; in fact this can be counterproductive, as we shall see later. It is, however, important to know the first steps of that journey. For Steve Shirley the first steps were to set up a network with just one other woman who was doing something similar; for the Zone Gallery it was to draw up a business plan for the new venture.

In summary, people will be ready for change if some combination of these four factors are present: external pressures, internal dissatisfaction, the presence of a vision, and a knowledge of the first practical steps. These factors do not need to be present in equal measures, but their combined effect must outweigh people's natural resistance to change.

A strategy for change

If an organization is ready for change, how is it best introduced? It is possible to draw a useful analogy between the introduction of a new idea, such as TQM, to an organization, and the introduction of a new product, such as a compact disc player, to a mass market. In both cases, individual responses will vary; some people will be enthusiastic straight away, others will take some convincing, some will take a lot of persuasion and others might never be convinced at all. Understanding how this works is crucial to the implementation of TQM, and that is why we now turn to look at the concepts behind the marketing of consumer products.

Product marketing experts divide people into four categories. Like many marketing theories, this is a big oversimplification, but it provides useful insights. The first of these categories comprises the *innovators*. This is a very small group of adventurous people who will try anything. Innovators were the first to use pocket calculators in the sixties, to wear flared trousers in the seventies and to use microwave cookers in the eighties. Sometimes they correctly mark the beginning of a much larger trend – as in the above examples – and sometimes they get it completely wrong; the few Sinclair C5 electric vehicles seen on the road were all driven by innovators. For this reason, innovators are regarded by others as somewhat quirky, even eccentric.

The second group is called the *early adopters*. Unlike the innovators, early adopters are widely respected and influential. Early adopters see how the innovators fare with a new product and then make an informed decision for themselves. This group is the most important so far as any new product is concerned. If the early adopters take it on then it has a very high chance of popular success.

The third group, the *majority* is said to comprise some 70 per cent of the population as a whole. This group takes their cue not from the manufacturers themselves, not from the innovators, but from the early adopters. Common sense reinforces this notion: in most cases you are more likely to buy a product if it is recommended to you by a friend whose judgement you trust, rather than on the basis of the manufacturer's own claims. Skilful marketeers take these three categories very seriously when launching new products. Flora margarine, for example, was initially available only in specialized health shops. In marketing terms, this was aiming it at innovators. Once it was established here, a campaign was aimed at a broader group of health conscious people. It became available – still at a premium price – in some supermarkets. This group of people were deemed to be the early adopters. Only when Flora was firmly established with this group was it then aimed at a mass market, as an everyday margarine at an everyday price.

Finally, marketeers identify a small group of people whom they label *laggards*. These people are probably best described as traditionalists. By and large laggards ignore trends and stick to what they know. They will continue to use vinyl LPs, long after CDs have become the standard.

It is important to realize that different people fit into different categories for different products; an individual might be an innovator when it comes to electronics, the first person with a laptop computer, or personal digital assistant; in the majority when it comes to fashion; and a laggard when it comes to food – meat and two veg only. How can this model shed light on the implementation of TQM?

Whoever first introduces TQM into the organization will be, in marketing terms, the innovator, and will be seen, at least so far as TQM is concerned, as somewhat eccentric. The innovator may well be tempted to convince everyone, as soon as possible, how wonderful TQM is. This approach will almost certainly fail. If the innovator is a department head, other department heads will find reasons why it can't work in their departments. If there is a certain amount of departmental rivalry, or even antagonism, then there will be even more resistance to the idea. If the chief executive doesn't proclaim his or her support, perhaps for fear of alienating the department heads, then TQM really is a non-starter. Even if the idea originates from the chief executive, there is a danger that it will be sabotaged by all the department heads, especially if they see TQM as a threat to their power or privileges. This phenomenon is known to chief executives as the soggy sponge effect; even if you have an idea which the majority of the staff like the sound of, it can often be foiled by the layer of management between you and the staff – the soggy sponge of departmental heads.

The TQM advocate should take a different strategy. First build up a small but very committed group of supporters – in marketing terms a group of early adopters. This should be done by talking about TQM in a way which encourages people to voice their concerns and think it through for themselves. As part of his strategy to introduce TQM into a UK branch of the American textiles company Millikens, Director Clive Jeanes led a seminar for senior managers. Participants were asked to work in small groups to list all the ways they could think of to empower their staff. One of the groups found it impossible to do the task and were very wary of having to report back that they didn't really understand what empowerment was. Their anxiety increased as the other groups seemed to have lots of ideas. When they reported back that they didn't really understand the concept of empowerment, to their surprise Clive Jeanes singled them out for special praise. One of the true signs of a quality organization, he argued, was that people were honest about what they didn't know. Had he criticized their efforts he probably would have alienated them; but by genuinely encouraging their honesty he had begun to create a core of TQM early adopters in the company.

The early adopters – whether they are a group of senior managers, or a quality council, or merely a group of interested staff – should be allowed the opportunity to convince themselves that TQM is worth investigating, not have it thrust down their throats. In particular the innovators should listen very carefully to the reasons for any resistance to the concept; any reservations the early adopters might have will be magnified at least tenfold by the rest of the organization.

Only when the early adopters are committed to TQM should an attempt be made to introduce it to the rest of the organization. If the organization is facing an immediate crisis, or if for some other reason everyone is ready for fast and drastic change, then TQM could be introduced in the form of a major launch. Usually, though, it is better to proceed in a less spectacular but more steadfast way. Often the next step is for the early adopters to take TQM into their own parts of the organization in whatever way seems appropriate. For some it will be by setting up a quality improvement team, for others by putting increased emphasis on measuring what customers want, for others by doing some team-building. At the same time, there should be some overall monitoring of the process by some kind of quality council.

Leadership style

A great deal has been written about leaders and leadership style. Some leaders appear to achieve results by acting very autocratically, using their formal authority and power to coerce others into action. This style does have certain advantages; it is quick, and it is certain, in that providing you have enough power you can be sure that your instructions will be followed. However, this approach is very poor at building commitment. There is the danger that things will be done differently as soon as the leader is not there to enforce them. At the other end of the spectrum is the democratic approach; the leader who discusses, listens and then moves forward only on the basis of consensus. Although most people see this as preferable to autocracy, this approach also has significant drawbacks. It is very time consuming and the outcome is much less certain. If the managing director says 'we will organize our factory this way', not only can this happen quickly, but it will be clear at the outset what the end result will be. If the department heads meet to try and reach consensus on how the factory will be organized, then not only will the decision take far longer – weeks or months rather than days – but it is not at all clear what they will finally agree. Such uncertainty can be very unsettling for all concerned. However, the democratic style does have two huge advantages over the autocratic approach. The level of commitment reached is far higher; the department heads may take a while to reach agreement, but when they do they are more likely to be committed to it than to the managing director's idea. Secondly, the democratic approach allows other people to develop skills and expertise for themselves.

Which style should be used by the leader who wishes to introduce TQM into an organization? There is no simple answer to this question, because there are so many variable factors to be considered: the nature of the business, the existing culture in the company, the wishes and expectations of staff. Nevertheless, research across a range of organizations which have successfully introduced TQM shows some common themes emerging. Leaders have tended to be fairly autocratic and inflexible when it comes to matters of principle – that customer needs are paramount, that integrity is vital – and very democratic when it comes to the way these principles are put into practice. In other words, such leaders are rigid in their principles but do an extraordinary amount of listening and working by consensus in order to implement them. Implementing TQM is rather like being in charge of a small sailing vessel in unpredictable weather. You must be absolutely sure of your final destination, but very flexible about the exact route to get there; you must be prepared to go on a new tack at each change of the winds and currents. That is why it is useful to explain the first practical steps toward a change, but unhelpful to map out the whole route at the very start. Not only does it reduce commitment, but given the unpredictable climate in which most changes take place, it is simply not possible to be sure of the whole route until the voyage is underway.

Having examined the general principles of change management, we now turn to some case studies to examine them in action. Like all the case studies in this book, the following examples are based on real organizations; only the names have been changed.

The big bang approach

Casterbridge Cinema is one of the country's leading independent cinemas. It shows a very wide variety of films from the very popular to the very obscure, in the comfortable surroundings of a 1930s Art Deco building. Although it could not survive commercially, it receives a grant from the local regional arts board in recognition of its imaginative programming and educational work. The cinema employs about twenty staff, some of them part time.

When a new director took over he decided that the cinema's future was secure only if it could find out what its customers wanted and deliver this. He began by commissioning some market research which confirmed that customers liked the choice of films and the general ambience of the cinema, but were dissatisfied with the amount of time they sometimes had to queue for tickets, and the state of the toilets. On the basis of this research, coupled with his strong commitment to equal opportunities, the director was able to raise money from a variety of sources for a major refurbishment programme. This included resiting the box office, giving wheelchair access to the auditorium and a complete refurbishment of the toilets and washrooms. All these changes were very much welcomed by staff, customers and funders.

The next steps were more difficult. The staffing structure was lopsided; there were too many projectionists and not enough 'front of house' staff – usherettes, box office staff and so on. One projectionist was made redundant and new front of house staff were taken on. In line with the new commitment to meeting customer needs the usherettes were renamed as customer service assistants (CSAs) and the box office staff, senior customer service assistants (SCSAs). The front of house manager became head of customer services. Apart from the director himself, no one supported this change of name.

Realizing that a change of name was not enough, the director began to investigate training for the CSAs and SCSAs in customer care, and he talked to a number of consultancy firms about this. One of these companies made a convincing case that what Casterbridge Cinema needed was not customer-care training but Total Quality Management. The consultant made a convincing case that mere training for staff who came into contact with customers was not enough; in order to satisfy external customers, he said, everyone in the organization had to deliver a quality service to all the internal customers as well. There should be TQM for all, not just customer care for a few. The director agreed that the consultancy firm should run two one-day seminars; each seminar would be attended by half of the staff.

The scene was now set for a major disaster. A good half of the staff were very young and overqualified for their jobs, but they were very interested in film. A number of these had a very cynical view of management; in fact, they felt that it was unnecessary to have a director and that arts organizations were best run as collectives. None of them was particularly dissatisfied with the present situation; apart from the low wage they had few complaints. They rather liked evenings when there were very few customers in; it gave them more time to be with those customers and chat with them. Although the director had a vision, it was not one which excited the staff much; they felt there was a danger of becoming too much like the Odeon over the road. In fact the only person supporting TQM was the director; he was the innovator and there was no critical mass of early adopters.

The consultant began the first seminar by introducing some of the key TQM concepts, including the idea of right first time and no checking. A long debate ensued in which everyone agreed it was vital to do lots of checking: if the box office returns weren't checked there was a danger that an SCSA could embezzle some of the takings; if the fire exits weren't checked every day there was a danger that they could be closed by the fire officer, and so on. The consultant changed tack and asked the participants to identify areas of waste and inefficiency. Some of the participants took this very personally and felt they were being criticized. At one point a CSA said that she felt that the office staff were a bit out of touch with what went on front of house; being in an office nine to five gave no impression of how difficult it was working in the evenings, dealing with drunkards or rude customers for example. The seminar left everyone feeling dissatisfied. The second seminar was better, but not much. Afterwards the director and consultant agreed that the cinema was not yet ready for TQM and that it should be abandoned for the time being.

With hindsight it is easy to see what went wrong. The staff at the cinema were not ready for change. Rather than trying to create a group of early adopters the director and consultant tried to convince everyone in one go. Finally neither the consultant nor the director were willing to listen to staff ideas about developing quality; instead, they tried to impose their own methods of right first time and no checking. The cinema's approach can be described as a big bang method – try to get everyone committed, immediately. This approach will always fail, and yet it is frighteningly common in many British organizations. It is tempting to speculate that there is a national characteristic which makes us generally resistant to change imposed upon us, but if we must implement change ourselves we always try the quick fix.

The critical mass approach

About a thousand people work at Kingsbere University. The senior management team consists of a vice-chancellor, four deans who lead the academic departments, and four directors of administrative departments. The original idea to introduce TQM into the university came from the dean of the business school. Although her colleagues were initially somewhat sceptical, the vice-chancellor was very supportive.

Initially, the big bang approach was used. The business school had recently done some work for a large manufacturing company that had successfully implemented TQM some years ago, and the dean negotiated for this company to lend the university four of its training officers. They came to the university and ran a series of half-day briefings for all 1,000 staff. The success of these briefings was mixed. Some of the administrative staff thought they were quite interesting, but found it hard to say how the ideas would work in a university. The reception from academic staff was generally much more hostile. Lecturers resented having to rearrange teaching to attend the briefings, and a number felt that this was just the latest bit of management jargon being imposed upon the university by an insensitive government. The training officers found the academics quite difficult to work with. As one participant said: 'If you hold up any concept academics will try to dissect it, critique it and generally rip it to shreds – that's what academics are trained to do.' The overall verdict on the briefings was that they had been interesting, but that absolutely nothing had changed as a result of them. The big bang approach had failed once again.

What was needed was a proper strategy. The university invited a dozen consultancy firms to tender for the implementation of TQM at Kingsbere. Ten of the firms put in bids, four made formal presentations, and one was selected. Merely going through this process gave the university a lot of ideas for the implementation strategy.

The consultants who were appointed first spent a few days talking to people at all levels and in all departments of the university. The purpose of this early diagnostic work was to ascertain whether the preconditions for TQM were in place, and to see what TQM activities might already be happening, if under a different name. There was good and bad news. On the one hand many of the academic staff rejected the notion of management, although paradoxically they respected most of the current managers. On the other hand there was some readiness for change. Most academic staff were aware of external pressures from government to be more competitive as an institution. Growing student numbers with no extra resources were causing internal dissatisfaction. Finally the knowledge of the first practical steps towards improved quality existed in the form of a body called the Cross Departmental Operations Group which had been running very effectively for two years. This group was effectively a quality improvement team; most recently it had done some excellent work in improving the way in which both teaching rooms and office accommodation had been allocated.

The next stage, as the consultants saw it, was to create a critical mass of early adopters. The consultants recommended that this group should be the senior management team itself – the vice-chancellor, deans and directors. The senior management team disagreed; they saw the key group as being the fifty or so heads of department who reported directly to them. A compromise was reached; the senior management team would spend a two-day residential seminar looking at TQM, and this would be followed by a one-day session, which would be run four times so all heads of department could attend. The agenda for the senior management team would cover customer expectations, measurement, teamwork, communication, organization for quality, reward systems and how to oversee the quality strategy. The agenda for the heads of department meetings concentrated on customer expectations, measurement and teamwork. At the end of both seminars participants were expected to go away and implement personal action plans. Dates were set for all these events.

Unfortunately the two-day residential seminar for the senior management team had to be rescheduled. Some of them felt that this was because members were genuinely too busy to give the event the attention it deserved on the originally agreed dates; others more cynically felt that one or two people weren't willing to face some of the more difficult issues the days might highlight, for example the lack of teamwork amongst members of senior management, and the widely held view that one of the deans was quite incompetent as a manager.

The first seminars for heads of department went very well. There were very high levels of involvement and commitment to the whole idea. Action plans were made. The senior management team seminar happened after two of the heads of department seminars. It also went well, although it was clear by the end that not all members fully understood the concepts. The next head of department seminar was also a success, in sharp contrast with the final one which was a disaster. The seminars had been deemed to be compulsory, so most of the participants who came on the last one had been trying to put it off as long as possible. All of the participants on the final seminar were strongly resistant to the notion of any management philosophy, and especially one which was, they felt, couched so strongly in the language of consumerism – customers, suppliers, measurement and so on. The fact that the previous seminars had gone well merely increased their resistance; they saw themselves as the last defenders of education and research in an institution which seemed to want to turn itself into some kind of factory. In marketing terms this group represented the laggards, those who were never going to be convinced by TQM. However the seminar provided the consultants with further information about some of the concerns which the rest of the university staff might have about TQM, especially those on the academic side. And despite the outcome of the last seminar, there was now a critical mass of perhaps forty early adopters, who by taking their action plans back to the departments would begin the process of introducing TQM to the university as a whole. Moreover, by listening carefully to the most vocal objectors – the laggards – the consultants had valuable information to help them plan the next stage of the implementation strategy.

Three months after the last of the seminars a conference was held for all university managers. Progress on action plans was reviewed. Although there had been little or no progress on about half of the plans, there had been satisfactory progress on the other half. Three of the departmental heads had led departmental purpose audits in their departments; many of the service departments had drawn up clearer specifications for what their internal customers wanted; and in the case of the reprographics department entirely new procedures had been written and implemented to replace the rather informal system of the person who shouts loudest gets their printing done quickest. In addition to celebrating the achievements to date, it was agreed to create the post of training manager for the university, and to set up and train a group of people to lead quality improvement teams. Finally, the conference decided to drop the label Total Quality Management to describe the work they were doing. They felt it smacked too much of quick-fix package to solve all the university's ills. Instead they talked about the University's Quality Improvement Philosophy.

It is now a year since the dean of the business school first persuaded her colleagues to look at TQM and there has been enormous progress. The library conducted a major survey of student and staff needs; a huge list was drawn up of current dissatisfactions and Pareto analysis was used to identify the key problems. As a result both the library opening hours and the layout of reference and study areas were completely overhauled. A quality improvement team looked at the difficulties course team leaders often had in timetabling courses which drew on lecturers from different departments. Its recommendations were welcomed and implemented by lecturers. Student surveys indicate that the university is now providing them with a better service than ever before, not only in terms of teaching, but also in areas like accommodation services and student counselling. The appointment of a training manager was a great success and has been followed up by a quality manager who co-ordinates the various quality improvement teams which operate at any given time.

Managing change

It is tempting to see the above case studies in terms of goodies and baddies – Kingsbere got it right and Casterbridge didn't. The reality of organizational life is more complex than that. While Casterbridge Cinema did fail to implement TQM some very positive things emerged from the exercise. As was recognized during the first seminar, communication between the office and front of house (the CSAs and SCSAs) was very poor. The seminar did have the effect of making the staff feel they were all part of one big team, partly by their common dislike of the consultant and his jargon-filled ideas. As a result a few staff from the office and from front of house met together informally and came up with a practical suggestion for improving communication. It was agreed that each of the SCSAs would spend one day a month working alongside the office staff. Had TQM been accepted, this same idea might have emerged from a quality improvement team, but the fact that it happened anyway is all to the good. Unintended outcomes of a change management process can often cause as much good – or harm – as the intended outcomes.

Kingsbere University did achieve success with its quality improvement programme, and in the light of that success it is easy to forget just how difficult the early stages were. Before the consultants had been brought in the initial 'big bang' approach had been fairly disastrous and the credibility of the business school dean had been severely damaged. She was perceived by some of her colleagues as rocking the boat in an unacceptable way. After the very first seminars the university's senior management team met to decide whether to involve outside consultants or drop the whole TQM idea. This meeting was extremely difficult for the dean of the business school, as it was touch and go as to whether her colleagues would allow consultants to be brought in. As one of the other deans asked, was this not simply a case of throwing good money after bad? The dean of management was at this point reminded of a quotation from Rosabeth Moss Kanter, to the effect that most successful changes look like disasters in the middle. Nevertheless, the senior management team did approve the use of consultants to implement TQM, and this probably would never have happened without the initial programme of seminars. Clarity and consensus are often preceded by uncertainty, confusion and controversy; new ideas are only good in retrospect.

It is tempting to think of organizational change like this:

It sometimes appears like this:

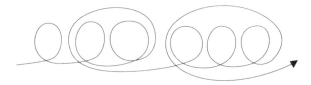

In reality it is more often like this:

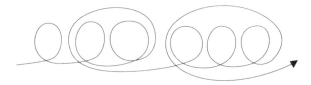

Fig. 10

Both Casterbridge and Kingsbere used external consultants to help implement TQM. There are many advantages to doing this: consultants can bring an outside perspective and the skills both of managing organizational change and of TQM itself. There are obviously drawbacks too: the cost and the risk of poor advice. Using consultants does make a difference and it is wise to consider external help with major organizational changes. If you do intend to use an external consultant you should always draw up a very clear written brief for what you would like the consultant to do, and then ask a number of different consultants to submit proposals. In this way, not only are you more likely to get the best consultant for your particular project, but, like Kingsbere, you have the opportunity to discover a number of alternative approaches.

5 Is TQM Right for Your Organization?

Despite its popularity, TQM has its detractors. It has been described as merely the latest fad, one of a long line of management fads which have lined the pockets of management consultants but failed to deliver anything substantial and worthwhile to organizations and people who work in them. Another line of attack is to accept that it can work in some settings – Japanese car factories and American retailers perhaps – but not in British companies. It is also said that TQM is just another device for managers to exploit the workers. It is now time to consider the case for TQM and these and other objections to it.

The positive side

At the end of the Second World War, the Japanese economy was in complete disarray. A number of initiatives were explored both by the Japanese government and by individual Japanese industrialists to find ways of rebuilding Japan's industrial base. One of these was to invite a young American statistician, W. E. Deming, to talk to them about his work in American armaments factories during the war. Deming had implemented a programme which was a curious mixture of employee participation and teamwork, coupled with very rigorous measurement and documentation of process. This combination had been extremely successful in increasing not only the amount of ordnance produced, but its reliability and quality. Deming's ideas were matched with some concepts that had long been part of traditional Japanese culture – a liking for things which were small, elegant and well crafted – to produce a manufacturing system which was later to be called Total Quality Management.

The next forty years saw Japanese industry moving from almost non-existence to dominating world markets. This is best illustrated by the growth of the Japanese car industry. In 1950 Japanese motor firms produced 30,000 vehicles a year, about one and a half days' production in the United States at that time. Most of these were not Japanese designs but American and British cars built under licence. Nissan, for example, had an agreement with Austin of England to make copies of the A40 and A50 models. By 1990 the tables had turned. Japanese companies now produce some 1.5 million cars each year. Over 100,000 a year are imported into the UK alone, and this number is restricted by a voluntary agreement. Rover, the only surviving volume British manufacturer, attributes its survival to a joint venture with Honda and the use of TQM and other Japanese working practices. As the recession of the early 1990s continues, amongst the few firms taking on new workers in Britain are Nissan and Toyota at their manufacturing plants in Sunderland and Derbyshire. Similar success stories could be told of Japanese firms in electronics and electrical goods. Much of this success is linked with the way TQM is used in these companies.

By the 1970s threats of Japanese competition, especially in cars and electronics, gave an incentive to American companies to look at TQM. Throughout the 1970s and 1980s a number of American organizations began to develop TQM techniques, not only in manufacturing but also in services and retailing. A good example of TQM ideas leading to great commercial success is given by Stew Leonard's grocery store. In 1969 the State of Connecticut decided to route a highway through the small dairy Stew Leonard had inherited from his father, so he decided to open a small grocery store. The original store offered only eight products, but Stew Leonard was driven by a desire to meet the needs of his customers to a degree that was then very rare for a grocer. By consistently applying a TQM philosophy he was able to expand the business. Today, 26 expansions later, Stew Leonard's is the top-grossing, highest-volume food store in the world. The store attracts 100,000 shoppers a week and has annual sales of over $100 million. It is mentioned in the Guinness Book of Records for the highest sales per square foot of any shop in the world.

The entire operation is ruthlessly orientated to pleasing customers. Although the product range is limited – about 750 items compared to the 15,000 conventional supermarkets stock – prices are 10 to 25 per cent lower than other food stores. There are enough check-out lines to ensure that no queue has more than three customers, and on the rare occasion that it does, free snacks and ice creams are offered to customers in the line. The store's slogan is 'Satisfy the customer; Teamwork gets it done; Excellence makes it better; Wow makes it fun'. In order to make shopping a fun experience there is a small farm in the car park, and store employees dressed as Disney characters wander around the store passing out balloons to children and telling shoppers about special offers. At one time the cash registers set off electronic mooing on purchases of over $100. One wall of the store is covered with over 7,000 photographs of customers holding Stew Leonard carrier bags at various locations around the world: the North Pole, the Great Wall of China, on the floor of the Pacific Ocean. Over ten years, an average customer will spend perhaps $50,000, hence another of Leonard's slogans, 'If I see a frown on a customer's face, I see $50,000 about to walk out the door.'

It was initially UK subsidiaries of American companies who brought TQM to Britain in the late 1970s. The success of these companies as compared to their British competitors led to TQM beginning to gain a hold in this country. The concepts of TQM have been used not only in the private sector, but also in the public and social welfare sectors, often to great effect. One of the best examples of TQM at work in the British public sector is given by the Post Office. In the mid 1980s the outlook for the Post Office was very poor. It had just been separated from the potentially very profitable telecommunications business. Predictions were made of a long-term decline in post in the light of competition from phone, fax and computer modems. In 1988 there was a long and acrimonious strike of postal workers and a parliamentary committee was criticizing the postal service which was delivering less than 60 per cent of first-class mail the next day. Soon after this, however, two Post Office executives visited North America to study TQM at work. They brought back some radical ideas for developing the postal service. To begin with, the entire management structure was overhauled; HQ staff were reduced from 2,000 to 200, and managers were encouraged to see themselves as coaches and enablers of front line staff. All 200,000 Post Office employees have taken part in quality training. The results of this have been dramatic. Over 90 per cent of first-class mail is now delivered the next day. This figure is the best in Europe; the German postal service, by way of contrast manages only 75 per cent. In terms of profitability the Post Office contributes some £200m each year to Treasury funds. Indeed, it is said by some commentators to be rather an embarrassment to certain Conservative government ministers who do not like to see such a successful organization operating in the public sector.

If the success of TQM were restricted to the Japanese car industry, the North American retail trade and the British Post Office it would be worth studying in some depth. As it is, thousands of organizations around the world have benefitted from TQM. Equally, many thousands of others have not. Now is the time to consider some of the possible reasons why.

TQM and national culture

It has sometimes been said that Stew Leonard's dairy store, with its emphasis on making shopping a fun experience, wouldn't work in Britain. Although that is probably true, it is to miss the point. TQM is not about giving the customer a fun experience, it is about giving the customer what he or she wants. In Connecticut that may be fun and low prices, elsewhere it may be something quite different. The Superquinn chain of food stores in Ireland owes a great deal to Stew Leonard's model. They too offer prices considerably below their direct competitors, they too make use of customer panels to develop and test new ideas. They too pioneered customer self-selection at a time when most other supermarkets offered only ready-packed fruit and vegetables. Whereas Stew Leonard fills his store with Disney characters and mooing cash registers, Superquinn gives its customers the extra features they want – an in-store delicatessen where customers can construct their own pizza for example. Both Stew Leonard's and Superquinn work to the same principle, that of giving their customers what they want; the application of those principles gives different results in different countries.

It may be the case that national cultures do affect, to a limited

degree, the ability of organizations to implement TQM programmes. If it is true that Japanese culture values perfection and
attention to detail then it will be easier to implement TQM in
such a culture than one which is happy to make do with
something rough and ready. Likewise, if it is true that North
American companies tend to be more informal and less hier-
archical than British ones, then TQM will be easier to implement
in the USA than in Britain. However, there is a danger in
attributing too much to the effects of national culture, as there is a
great deal of evidence to show TQM successfully at work in a
wide variety of national settings. In particular, Japanese companies like Nissan and Toyota seem able to implement TQM
even more successfully in British plants with British workers
than they do in some of their domestic factories.

Is TQM right for every organization?

Some of the advocates of TQM – books, management consultants – give the impression that TQM has something to offer
every organization. This is misleading. There are some organizations where TQM would be positively harmful. One of these is
Simon Byrne's pine stripping business. He buys old furniture
from a variety of sources – auctions, house clearances – dips it
into a tank of chemicals which strips off the old paints, repairs and
restores it and sells it. Some of his customers buy a lot; one Dutch
man regularly arrives with a large pantechnicon and buys as
much as he can fit in. Other customers might buy the odd stool
once in a blue moon. Others will bring in a few doors simply to
be dipped into the tank. Simon occasionally employs other staff
to work the tank, do joinery work, or – in the case of the sixth-
former who comes in on Saturdays – to keep the place reasonably
clean and tidy. The business is run in a very informal way. It has
no mission statement, no business plan, no job descriptions and
no written procedures. As Simon admits, it is run far from
efficiently. 'For a start I don't really need to come in on Saturdays
– I'm sure I don't make any money then. I just like it – you've got
a chance to potter around a bit which you can't do in the week.
On the other hand I've got the flexibility to shut up shop and get
home early to spend time with my family. I've no idea who my

customers are or where they come from – they just seem to turn up. So far as my pricing is concerned, I just try to make a bit on whatever I do – so I tend just to add a bit on to whatever I've paid in the first place. I'm sure that means that I overcharge desperately on some things and undercharge on others, but I don't really care. If I like a piece of furniture I'll pay over the odds, and if I really like a customer I'll let them have stuff a bit cheaper.'

At first glance, it appears that Simon has sacrificed commercial success for quality of life. He certainly has the latter, he enjoys his work and is a popular member of his local community which includes many of his customers and suppliers. Byrne's Pine Stripping is also commercially very successful; behind the façade of chaos is a very well thought out strategy. Simon's method of pricing – putting a small mark-up on the cost price – does mean that customers occasionally get some really outstanding bargains. The prospect of a bargain – even on only one visit in ten – is an important factor in the antique furniture business, and gives Simon's business a huge competitive advantage. Likewise, the clutter of old furniture in the old mill in which the business lives may offend TQM principles of keeping inventory to a minimum, but makes perfect sense in a business where stock does not depreciate, but increases in value over time. Simon enjoys both quality of life and commercial success.

TQM has very little to offer Byrne's Pine Stripping. Simon has a good intuitive feel for what his customers want, and where he hasn't he doesn't care. Anything TQM could add in terms of efficiency would be a net loss to Simon, his staff and customers who are very happy with the way the organization is now. Whilst this style of operation would be quite unacceptable in other settings, it works well for many small organizations where greater efficiency would not necessarily lead to greater effectiveness.

At the opposite end of the business spectrum from Byrne's Pine Stripping must be IBM, the computer giant. Its annual turnover of $64 billion is larger than the GNP of some national states. It employs 300,000 people world-wide. IBM was one of the first companies to introduce TQM in both the United States and the UK. IBM's Havant manufacturing plant introduced quality circles in the 1960s. Many TQM techniques were in fact developed by IBM, in particular the use of departmental purpose audits. The company's commitment to TQM continues to this day. However, in 1993 IBM announced that it had made a loss of $9 billion. This represents the biggest loss made by any business ever. What went wrong? Most of this $9 billion was spent on restructuring the business. Part of this was the redundancy costs for the 40,000 staff who were no longer needed, but a substantial part was spent trying to refocus IBM's business from mainframes to microcomputers. TQM had helped IBM to be efficient but not effective. To oversimplify things somewhat, IBM did a superb job of producing large mainframe computers which are becoming increasingly irrelevant as networks of microcomputers supersede them. It could be argued that IBM was not using TQM enough, that TQM should have helped IBM to see that its customers wanted microcomputers, not mainframes. But this is asking a lot of TQM. If the organization is broadly heading in the right direction – in other words if it has the right strategy – TQM can help to implement that strategy efficiently and effectively. But if the direction is wrong, TQM is not the best tool to turn the organization around. To be effective, IBM had completely to alter its strategic direction; TQM had not helped it to do this.

Byrne's Pine Stripping and IBM illustrate two important points about TQM. First, TQM should not be applied willy-nilly to every organization. Some organizations are able to operate very successfully without it. In fact if Simon Byrne paid management consultants to introduce TQM into his business it would probably destroy it. Second, TQM is not enough to guarantee organizational success. For many years, IBM was held as an example of all that is best in large multinational corporations, and much of this was due to the application of TQM. But this was not enough to keep IBM profitable. For IBM, as for many organizations, other techniques are needed too. In some cases, nothing will save an organization from decline or extinction. As we have seen in the previous chapter, changes in the external environment play a big part in the success of many organizations.

Is the climate right?

However carefully they are nurtured, it is just not possible to grow daffodils in polar regions. TQM is similar: it cannot be implemented unless the organizational climate is right. In this section we look at those aspects of organizational climate which are prerequisites to any TQM initiative. Since TQM is essentially a management philosophy, it is bound to fail unless there is a reasonable degree of trust in the organization's management. There are three components to this trust: an acceptance of the concept of management, the integrity of managers, and the competence of managers.

Most organizations have a formal management structure. In small organizations there will be the boss and a small group of staff or volunteers. In large organizations there will be a whole pyramid of hierarchy: chief executive, directors, senior managers, middle managers, supervisors, staff, apprentices and people on government training schemes. Whether or not individual managers are liked or disliked there is usually an acceptance that some form of management is necessary; someone has to set direction, co-ordinate work, make the tough decisions and so on. However, in some organizations this is not the case; staff see the managerial role as either unnecessary or fulfilling a very limited administrative function. This view was best put to me by a senior lecturer in a university. Lecturers, he explained to me, were professionals. This meant they made decisions on the basis of their professional integrity. Not only were managers unnecessary – how can someone judge my performance as a teacher or researcher if they lack my subject expertise? – but positively harmful, since they threatened the notion of academic freedom. As soon as we accept the notion that any manager has a right to control an academic's right to explore new areas of research, then we are one step nearer a police state where freedom of thought and expression is under threat. This lecturer found it impossible to view his work in terms of customers and suppliers; his job was the enhancement of human knowledge.

While this avowedly anti-managerial stance was not shared by all his colleagues in the university, the view that professionals should be left to practise their profession, unhindered by considerations of management, is very widespread. It is expressed by lawyers, doctors, social workers, teachers and charity workers, the people who provide many important social welfare services. While they hold this view, TQM is unlikely to find fertile ground within their organizations. Neither is such an anti-managerial stance confined to the professions. Much of the current commercial success of Rover cars is attributed to the introduction of TQM by its chairman Graham Day. Less credit is given to his predecessor, Michael Edwardes, who was generally seen to have had a much more confrontational style. However, after many years of a motor industry where union powers were strong and management powers comparatively weak, Michael Edwardes did re-establish the right of managers to manage, even if it was in a style which has been described as 'grab them by the scruff of the neck and their hearts and minds will follow'. Whilst there remain differing views as to whether the diminution of union power at Rover has been a good thing or a bad thing, the fact remains that it would not otherwise have been possible to introduce TQM into the company.

Simply believing in the principle of management is not enough; managers must be seen to act with integrity. Organizations who have successfully implemented TQM have very high ethical standards, and indeed often publish guidelines for staff. IBM for example issues a statement of ethical principles to all its staff which covers such things as company policy on gifts from customers or suppliers (they must all be returned to the donor). Unfortunately it is easy to find business illustrations of Lord Acton's famous comment that 'power tends to corrupt and absolute power corrupts absolutely'. In recent times the biggest business scandals to hit the headlines have been Robert Maxwell's use of individual pension funds to boost his own business, and the allegation that British Airways conducted a 'dirty tricks' campaign against rival airline Virgin. While these are the stories that hit the headlines, less dramatic lapses of honesty are very common indeed within organizations; managers who claim slightly more expenses than they are entitled to, who pilfer office stationery for personal use, or who simply lie to get out of difficult situations. It seems that people feel more able to be dishonest in an organizational setting then they do at home.

People who wouldn't dream of stealing pens from a neighbour's house feel able to take home office stationery for their children to play with. Often there is a kind of group pressure – if everyone uses the office phone for private calls why shouldn't I?

Another side of the integrity issue is the perks afforded to managers. While there is a general trend towards 'single status' companies where all employees share the same canteen, pension rights and perks such as staff discounts, there are still many organizations where managers enjoy privileges which are perceived to be unfair by many staff. There are, for example, two major child care charities in the UK who have strict guidelines on the allocation of company cars. In the first, cars are allocated to any member of staff whose job involves more than a certain amount of travel each year, irrespective of status. The car is always the same small and economical vehicle. In the second organization cars are allocated partly on the basis of need, but also in terms of status: a regional fundraiser who travels 40,000 miles a year is allocated a very small hatchback, a middle manager a family saloon, and a senior director – who may do almost no travelling at all as part of the job – an estate car. If either organization is keen to introduce TQM, it will clearly be easier in the first organization. Executive perks are rare in the social welfare sector, but are common elsewhere. I was once asked to do some consultancy for a company where the senior managers had heated garages for their company cars while staff had to draw lots for limited space in the company car park. They were surprised to be told that any TQM effort was doomed to failure while such obvious and unnecessary inequalities existed. While there is a general acceptance that managers should earn more than staff, there is a question about how great the differentials should be. Organizations which give senior executives substantial awards while implementing pay freezes for the rest of the staff are certainly going to find it more difficult to create a climate where everyone works as a team.

Acting with integrity is not just about not breaking the law or not abusing your position of power; it is about meaning what you say every time. A manager who responds to a request with 'I'll see what I can do' is not acting with integrity if he knows that change isn't really possible. TQM puts much stress on making promises and keeping to them. If anyone promises a certain level of service then they must stick to that promise. This aspect of integrity is particularly important in situations where it is difficult for the customer to make an informed choice. If I go to one doctor about my back and he prescribes aspirin, and another recommends an urgent and potentially dangerous operation, how am I to choose? The only safeguard in these circumstances is the integrity of the doctor.

A recent survey of European managers asked what attributes they would value in a manager, and how their present chief executive compared with this ideal. Integrity and honesty were near the top of the list of desirable qualities, but less than half of those interviewed felt that their own chief executive acted with integrity and honesty. It is possible that organizations are structured in a way which actually rewards behaviour which is less than 100 per cent honest. It is more common for them to promote people who toe the company line than it is to promote those who tell the truth, particularly if it is unpalatable to senior managers. The temptations for managers to act, if not dishonestly, then with less than a total commitment to integrity, are very great. If you were a senior manager choosing between an immediate personal gain – getting a big new office with a wonderful view – or the possibility of a long-term shared gain – improved organizational effectiveness through TQM – which would you choose?

The lower the organization's ethical standards, the lower the likelihood that TQM will be successful. If managers break their promises to staff, there is a powerful role model and justification for staff to break promises to customers. If managers provide themselves with excessive perks for short-term benefit, there is no motivation for staff to be concerned with long-term customer satisfaction. TQM cannot be introduced into this type of environment.

An acceptance of the management role and a belief in their integrity is not enough for TQM to be successfully implemented; managers must also have the skills to do so. Much has been written about the skills of managers, and many of the skills needed to be an effective manager day-to-day are applicable to TQM. In this section I want to highlight skills in four areas which are especially pertinent to any manager who is serious about implementing TQM into his or her organization. The first of these areas concerns analytical skills. TQM provides managers with some tools of analysis – fishbone charts and Pareto analysis for example – but the manager must have the skills to use them. Good analytical thinking involves an ability to understand the significance both of small details and of the big picture. A good example of this is given by Omega, the Swiss watch manufacturers. Until the 1960s Swiss companies dominated the world market for wrist-watches. Then, in the early 1970s, Omega noticed a very small decline in the sale of Swiss wrist-watches in North America. Good analytical thinking enabled them to notice the small details – the fact that the dip in sales had occurred in California and was now spreading to other parts of the USA – and to see the big strategic implications of this: the development of digital watches which had begun in Palo Alto, California would soon have an enormous impact on the sales of wrist-watches everywhere. As a result Omega was able to respond accordingly.

The second skill area concerns the ability to create a readiness for change. Perhaps the most important aspect of this is the ability to create an inspiring vision. This in turn hinges largely on the creativity of the individual manager. Creativity can be developed and learnt. There are techniques for developing creativity such as brainstorming, and formal educational programmes such as training in lateral thinking, developed by Edward de Bono and others. The biggest obstacle to creativity is the belief that it is somehow inherent and cannot be learnt.

The third skill area required for successful implementation is that of interpersonal skills. Managers need to be excellent at listening, questioning, giving and receiving feedback, and influencing – telling, persuading, negotiating, problem solving and facilitating. The problem here is not that people believe these skills cannot be learnt, it is that many managers feel they do not need to learn them. It is a curiosity of human nature that people are happy to admit they can't understand figures, or computers, but are usually loath to admit they are bad listeners or cannot accept feedback. Yet these skills are crucial to the implementation of any change management process, and especially to the implementation of TQM. Without the ability to listen and question, managers will never discover what their customers want. Without the ability to deal with feedback and influence, managers will never involve their workforce in delivering what customers want.

There is one final characteristic of managers who successfully implement TQM, that is, an ability to manage their own development. They have an accurate perception of their own strengths and weaknesses, because they are willing to ask for feedback and listen to it. They have an understanding of their own learning style; do they learn best by doing, observing, thinking or planning? They have a grasp of the variety of learning methods which are available to them; not just courses but more creative methods of development such as secondments, distance learning, special projects, mentoring and so on. In effect, they are applying TQM's philosophy of continuous improvement to themselves.

Moral issues

In summary, it is fair to say that TQM has a great deal to offer most, but not all, organizations. Organizations which do want to use it must consider very carefully whether the climate in the organization is right for the implementation of TQM, and in particular whether the integrity and honesty which TQM demands of managers exists. Does this mean that TQM occupies the moral high ground of management philosophies? The answer to this is almost but not quite. There is one aspect of TQM as it is currently practised which is less than wholesome, and that is TQM's obsession with external customers.

Outside Stew Leonard's grocery store there is a three-ton chunk of granite into which is chiselled, 'Rule 1: The customer is always right. Rule 2: If the customer is wrong, see rule 1.' What about customers who are rude or aggressive? Are employees expected just to grin and bear it? To put too much emphasis on customers is to ignore the other people involved in the organization, and in particular the employees. A hotel chain recently ran a series of newspaper advertisements explaining its commitment to customer service. One of these advertisements told the story of a hotel guest who found himself unable to find a taxi to the airport early one morning. One of the hotel staff, who was just coming to the end of her night shift, offered to take him there in her own car. The point of the advertisement was that the employees of this hotel went to very great lengths to ensure that customers were not only satisfied with the service, they were delighted with it. While this is very satisfactory from the customer's point of view, what about the employee's? Presumably on the occasion described the particular employee was happy to give up some of her free time, but would she be happy to do this on a regular basis if customers came to expect this level of service as a matter of course? Do other employees feel pressure to give this commitment?

A number of motor manufacturers who have introduced TQM make use of a particular system often called the 'Help Lamp'. A wire running the whole length of the production line can be pulled at any time by a worker who has a concern about quality. This activates a siren and flashing light which draws the attention of a supervisor who can investigate the cause of the concern. If necessary the entire production line is halted until the quality problem is resolved. The rationale for this system is clear: rather than employing quality controllers to check things when it is too late, every worker feels that he or she is responsible for quality, one of the principle aims of TQM. In practice, however, such a system can put workers under a great deal of strain. Workers can feel that comparatively trivial errors are highlighted in a very dramatic way if someone further down the line signals the alarm. Moreover, any production line which makes use of the Help Lamp too often is deemed incompetent, and so 'downstream' workers often feel they must correct errors made by 'upstream' workers rather than pulling the wire – or allowing it to be pulled by workers 'downstream' from them. From the workers' point of view the Help Lamp system can be just as oppressive as a supervisor standing immediately behind, watching their every move.

By focusing so strongly on the needs of external customers, there is the danger that TQM may lead to poor treatment of employees. This danger is tempered somewhat by the TQM philosophy that the best way to deliver quality to external customers is to deliver quality to every internal customer in the customer–supplier chain. In theory at least, TQM should treat internal customers – staff – with as much consideration as external customers. However, internal customers do not have the choice which external customers usually have, and so the potential for mistreatment (as the Help Lamp example shows) is always present.

Also of cause for concern is the danger that TQM's obsession with external customers may lead to very poor treatment of suppliers. Whenever large and powerful organizations use small and comparatively powerless firms as suppliers there is the danger that the suppliers will be treated badly. Many organizations in the private, public and social welfare sector use contract cleaning companies. These companies often pay extremely low wages and offer very poor conditions of employment. Many of them would like to pay staff more, but feel unable to because of commercial pressure. When the supplier is based in a developing country, there are real dangers of exploitation. To take but one example, many of the handmade carpets sold in the UK are manufactured in the Indian state of Uttar Pradesh. It is estimated that of the 100,000 young boys working in the carpet making industry, many are effectively slaves, sleeping on the premises, terrorized by the loom owners, working fifteen hours a day in dark, airless and extremely hot mud-brick huts with no real meal breaks.and minimal or no wages. Many of the products we take for granted in the West – including chocolate, tea, coffee, fruit – originate from exploitative conditions in developing countries.

It must be stressed that TQM is not explicitly exploitative; it does not advocate using slave labour or minimal wages to drive down costs. The problem with TQM is what it doesn't say. By focusing only on external customers there is no guidance for organizations to consider their responsibilities towards their other stakeholders, the people who are affected by the enterprise. Organizational stakeholders include not only customers, employees and suppliers, but also owners, and members of the local community. TQM's failure to acknowledge the role of these groups is a serious lacking; a response to this is considered in the next chapter.

6 Beyond TQM

Although TQM is sometimes described as the latest management fad, it has been practised by organizations, in various forms, for the last forty years. What of the future? Will TQM be the guiding philosophy for organizations in the next forty years? The short answer to this question has to be no. TQM is extremely difficult to implement and provides little help for organizations who wish to take account of the needs of all their stakeholders. Moreover there is a growing cynicism towards any package which purports to be 'the answer' to organizational effectiveness. However, many of the ideas on which TQM is based will be more important than ever. The concept of quality, for example, will become even more crucial than it is today. All organizations have customers, and the expectations of these customers will continue to increase. Products which were once considered luxury goods, such as telephones, televisions and washing machines, are now considered essential (at least in the West). Services which were once available only to the very wealthy, are now aspired to by all. There will be increasing pressure on organizations of all types to deliver higher and higher levels of quality.

If quality will continue to be important in the future, how will it be delivered? A new set of approaches to quality is emerging which I shall call Quality Improvement. It will have many similarities to TQM, but some important differences. Like TQM, Quality Improvement will be possible only if the organization pays careful attention to its ethical standards. This will go beyond honesty and integrity to consideration of respect for individuals, communities and the environment. High ethical standards are sometimes thought to be desirable but too idealistic in the real world. In a tough economic climate, it is sometimes said, the only way to survive is to 'play dirty' on occasions. In this chapter we'll look at examples of organizations which achieve their competitive advantage through ethical principles, and examine the notion that in an increasingly complex world, while short-term gains are to be had by acting unethically, long-term achievement is possible only by the application of high ethical standards.

Quality Improvement will differ from TQM in that it will explicitly address the needs not just of customers but of all organizational stakeholders – employees, suppliers, owners, local communities. This is clearly morally desirable; many people have qualms about TQM's obsession with customers only. Moreover I will argue in this chapter that as the nature of organizational forms becomes more complex, it simply becomes illogical to distinguish between customers and other stakeholders. Unlike TQM which is very much a philosophy for managers, Quality Improvement will be a philosophy for everyone. There is a logical argument for this. Increasingly the distinction between managers and staff which once made sense in many traditional manufacturing industries no longer makes sense in many organizations today. I will also give examples of organizations which attribute their success to a culture of empowerment where all employees take responsibility for the success of the enterprise. Finally, we will consider the implementation of Quality Improvement. TQM's emphasis on commitment from all and company-wide improvement often backfires. Quality Improvement will take a different tack; the emphasis on implementation will be very much on individual and local initiatives. Paradoxically, this makes it more likely that it will spread throughout the organization as a whole.

Ethics

The word 'ethics', like the word 'quality', is used in many different ways. What does the word mean in the Quality Improvement sense? What do we mean when we say an individual or organization is acting ethically? One component of ethical behaviour is honesty – telling the truth. If you say you are going to do something, do it. As we have seen in the previous chapter, this attribute is often missing in organizational life and is a major reason for the failure of TQM initiatives. An inflexible commitment to truth and honesty is even more important in

Quality Improvement. However, ethical behaviour involves more than honesty; an organization could, for example, be very honest about the fact that it employs staff on low wages in terrible conditions. Ethical behaviour also involves respect for individuals.

The moral desirability of respect for individuals is partly enshrined in the notion of equal opportunities. Most UK organizations would subscribe to the notion that they treat all employees fairly, irrespective of race, gender or marital status. The days in which female bank employees were expected to resign when they married are long gone. It is in fact illegal to discriminate on these grounds. Many organizations go beyond the legal requirement of fair treatment. For example, as part of their equal opportunities policies, many banks now offer career break opportunities for women employees. These enable women to take a number of years at home caring for children, with the guarantee of their old job when they return. From a strictly business point of view, this makes good sense. The skills and commitment of that member of staff could otherwise have been lost. Many organizations – particularly in the public and social welfare sectors – take equal opportunities and respect for individuals very seriously. As well as being morally desirable and legally necessary, it enables the organization to operate more effectively. Equal opportunities is of course only one aspect of respect for individuals. Nevertheless, organizations which take equal opportunities seriously are more likely to have regard for broader aspects of respect for individuals.

Ethical behaviour also takes into account the needs of people in the local community. When an organization sets up in a particular locality, it will have an impact on that community. This can be very positive. It can provide jobs; contribute to the welfare of that community by its support of local arts groups and charities; and even add to the physical resources of that community. This last idea is often described by local authorities as 'planning gain'; private sector companies are given planning permission to build a new shop or factory on condition that they also build a new community centre or access roads. Unfortunately, the impact of a new business in the locality can also be very negative, bringing with it higher road traffic flows, less green space and higher prices for local people. Similarly, when an organization chooses to leave a locality, the impact can be good or bad; former inaccessible land could be a valuable community resource or simply an abandoned and dangerous eyesore. The consequences of lost jobs are likely to be more critical still. Organizations clearly cannot make decisions about opening or closing new workplaces solely in terms of the effects on the local community; but for both ethical and business reasons it is important to be serious about taking them into account.

The final component of ethical behaviour is a concern with the physical environment. The greenhouse effect describes the phenomenon by which certain gases accumulate in the upper atmosphere and retain heat. This leads to a gradual warming of the Earth's atmosphere which will inevitably lead to massive changes in climatic patterns: floods, droughts, storms and crop failures. The accompanying rise in sea levels could make large areas of the UK uninhabitable. No one knows for sure how quickly this will happen, but the Intergovernmental Panel on Climate Change agreed that the current rate of warming was about 1°C every 30 years, enough to produce drastic changes within a lifetime. Over 50 per cent of global warming is caused by one greenhouse gas, carbon dioxide. A quarter of the increase in carbon dioxide is attributable to deforestation and three-quarters to the burning of fossil fuels such as coal, oil and gas. Therefore every organization which uses paper or energy – in other words practically every organization – is contributing to global warming.

Other environmental concerns are more likely to be industry-specific. Any organization which uses or produces chlorofluorocarbons (CFCs) is contributing towards the depletion of the ozone layer, which shields us from the full effects of the sun's ultraviolet (UV) radiation. Greater levels of UV severely affect plant growth and human health. Sulphur dioxide from burning coal and oil and nitrogen oxide from vehicle exhausts form acid rain, which leads to the destruction of life in freshwater lakes, stunting of crops and the erosion of buildings. More local environmental disasters frequently hit the headlines. When the Exxon Valdiz oil tanker ran aground in Prince William Sound, Alaska, bird life suffered 300,000 casualties. More than 10,000 humans died as a result of the release of methyl isocynate from the Union Carbide factory in Bhopal, India in 1984; a further 80,000 have been seriously affected.

Why should organizations concerned with quality improvement take account of environmental matters? While there are clearly moral reasons, to do with the long-term prospect for our planet, there are also very clear business reasons for so doing. Where customers have a choice, many prefer to receive services and products from environmentally concerned organizations. The success of the Body Shop in the UK is one example of this. The Body Shop sells soaps and cosmetics which have not been tested on animals, and is run in a way that is environmentally friendly; shop staff are provided with company bicycles to encourage them to leave their cars behind, for example. The success of the Body Shop has influenced competitors like Boots to stock similar environmentally friendly ranges. Another example is the rise of ethically based investments, such as pension funds which do not invest in companies with a poor environmental record. As well as being good for an organization's image, environmental concern can make immediate financial gains. All new Sainsbury's supermarkets are built in accordance with strict environmental guidelines. There are no central heating boilers; heat is recycled from the freezers and refrigerators into the offices and shopfloor. These stores need 40 per cent less energy than a comparable conventional supermarket and are therefore cheaper to run. In addition, refrigerators are constructed in such a way as to minimize CFC emissions, and stores are equipped with CFC 'sniffers' which sound the alarm if CFCs in the air exceed a certain amount. This also makes good business sense in the light of the fact that there is soon likely to be legislation restricting the emission of CFCs. Further evidence that environmental concern can lead to economic success is given by the US multinational 3M. In 1975 it introduced its 3P programme – Pollution Prevention Pays. Through redesign of both products and production methods, by 1990 3M had reduced solid wastes by 400,000 tonnes, air pollutants by 122,000 tonnes and water pollutants by 16,000 tonnes. In so doing the company saved some $482m.

Meeting the needs of all stakeholders

TQM is obsessed with customers. Despite the notion that employees simply treat each other as internal customers, there is the danger that this obsession leads to a focus on external customers at the expense of other organizational stakeholders, especially employees and suppliers. Leaving aside ethical considerations, this is often unsatisfactory from a logical point of view. Consider the distinction between customers and suppliers. This may make sense in a manufacturing context, where raw materials come in one end and pass along the links of a customer–supplier chain to emerge as finished products for external customers at the other. In other settings, however, the distinction makes much less sense. If Heinz offers to donate £100,000 to the Save the Children Fund in exchange for being able to use the Save the Children logo on its tins of beans, who is supplying whom? Is Heinz supplying SCF with money or SCF supplying Heinz with good publicity for which it has paid £100,000? If a manager provides support and guidance to her team members in return for information about the work they have done, who is the customer and who the supplier? In these and many other situations it makes more sense to view the relationship as a partnership; it is important for each party to make clear what they can offer to and expect of the other. Rather than seeing relationships in terms of customers and suppliers, Quality Improvement will view them in terms of partnerships. In any given transaction, it will be important to identify the needs of both partners and find ways of maximizing the benefit to both within the overall context. There used to be a chain of hardware stores in Canada where the staff wore roller skates. When a customer placed an order at the counter, the staff member would skate off as fast as he could to find the relevant item. This is the TQM approach: find out what the customer wants and deliver it. The Quality Improvement approach is to look at what both sides want and to maximize the benefit to both. It is this kind of thinking which lead to the self-service shop, where the customer effectively takes on some of the employees' responsibilities of fetching and carrying, but in a way which is to everyone's benefit.

The concept of partnerships is particularly relevant if we consider the likely organizational forms of the future. At present most organizations consist of a fairly fixed group of employees, most of whom are employed on a permanent, full-time basis. In the future, most organizations will consist of a very small central core of permanent employees, a large number of partner organizations who are contracted to do much of the work of the organization, and a pool of temporary workers who are employed on very short-term contracts as they are needed. A number of such tripartite organizations already exist, for example, many local authorities employ only a small core staff and contract out functions such as street cleaning and leisure provision. Temporary workers are employed at busy times in youth clubs, playschemes and so on. A similar pattern is being followed by many private sector companies who contract out non-core functions, and employ casual staff when demand merits it.

This form of organization has many advantages. Contracting out ensures that tasks are being carried out by experts in that field, and so the quality of work is higher. Employing casual staff produces an automatic cost saving, employers need pay no National Insurance, sick pay, holiday pay, pension or redundancy pay. The greater flexibility means that organizations can be more responsive to their customers. It is no wonder that many organizations, from manufacturing companies to high street retailers, from hospital trusts to social service departments are going down this route, often with the encouragement of government legislation. This flexibility is also valued by many people who do not want a full-time job. Many people with responsibility for child care, for example, welcome the chance to be able to earn an income and be at home when the children return from school.

There are however significant drawbacks to this structure, both for the individual and for the organization. When organizations contract out services, they invariably expect those tasks to be performed more cheaply; this tends to lead to lower wages. When Barclay's Bank recently contracted out its cleaning services, pay rates for cleaners fell by half. Of course not all organizations contract out only low-paid services; many companies, for example, contract out their staff training to well-paid management consultants. But the majority of services which are contracted out do tend to offer lower rates of pay than the equivalent in-house facility. Cost cutting is after all one of the reasons for contracting out the service. Directly employed casual staff are in an even more vulnerable position than the employees of contractors. The burden of market risk which was once born by the organization itself has been shifted to the casually employed individual. Such casual staff are obliged to shoulder periodic spells of unemployment and low income as a precondition of work, while the organization saves money. Job security is available only to a comparatively small number of people who have permanent contracts as core employees. The consequences of this could be a large underclass of mainly unskilled workers who rely on a series of short-term jobs. Although less obvious, there are disadvantages for the organization too. Contracting out any service may save money in that a contractor may be able to perform the service more efficiently and cheaply than the organization which is offering the contract. However, there are the costs of drawing up the tender brief, inviting bids for the tender, selecting the contractor and liaising with them over the long term. These transaction costs may outweigh any savings made. In general, the more adversarial the contracting process, the more the transaction costs will be. There is also the problem of disappearing demand. The survival of most private sector companies depends on customers buying goods and services. If the majority of people in the market are employed only on a casual basis, they may be more inclined to save their money against the risk of prolonged future unemployment than to spend it in the short term.

TQM does not address these problems directly; its focus is merely on the external customers. Quality Improvement, however, takes explicit account of all organizational stakeholders: contractors and casual staff, as well as permanent employees and traditional suppliers. Stakeholder theory has a long history, especially in the USA where many organizations express their formal commitment to meeting the needs of employees, suppliers and local communities, as well as to customers and shareholders. Recent research by John Kotter and James Heskett of Harvard Business School shows that this approach makes excellent commercial success. The research was initially concerned with the link between corporate culture and economic success. The authors calculated a 'culture strength indicator' for 200 big American firms, and then tried to correlate it with economic performance over an eleven-year period. Their initial findings were that a strong corporate culture was as likely to lead to failure as to success. This should be no surprise; a strong organizational culture can lead to arrogance and be an obstacle to change. The researchers then went on to identify which precise aspects of corporate culture did lead to improved performance. All the highest performing firms in their survey shared one characteristic: they did not let short-term concerns for profit override their long-term concern for the welfare of all stakeholders. In fact the twelve firms in the survey whose culture most valued all stakeholders increased their net profits by an average of 70 per cent each year over the eleven-year period.

A philosophy for everyone

TQM makes a very clear distinction between managers and staff. Managers plan, co-ordinate and control, and staff actually do the work. In TQM terms, it is the role of managers to remove the barriers which prevent staff from doing good work. Most quality problems, according to TQM, are caused by managers failing to remove these barriers, rather than by staff themselves. In fact Deming goes so far as to say that 94 per cent of quality problems are caused by managers, not by staff. In manufacturing and retailing – the settings where TQM was developed – the distinction between managers and staff is very clear. In many other types of organization it is not. As we have already seen, many professional organizations do not make a rigid distinction between those who plan, co-ordinate and control, and those who actually carry out the work. In many organizations, although there might be a distinction in terms of hierarchy – managers are paid more – this distinction does not apply to function; everyone in the organization spends some of their time actually 'doing' and some of their time 'planning, co-ordinating and controlling' the work of others (or at least attempting to).

Rather than seeing this blurring of roles as disadvantageous, Quality Improvement encourages this trend. Unlike TQM, which encourages the distinction between managers and staff, Quality Improvement encourages everyone to act as if they had full responsibility for their part of the organization. This concept is well expressed by the term *intrapreneurship*. Most people are familiar with the term entrepreneur: someone who initiates a new independent enterprise, develops and nurtures it. The entrepreneur faces the challenges of obtaining financial backing, and of meeting the demands of external customers. Entrepreneurs often don't have any formal authority over the people they wish to influence – bankers, donors, partners or staff. They influence by virtue of their vision and skills. The entrepreneur may be motivated by the prospect of financial gain, by philanthropy, by an enthusiasm for the product or service, or by other factors. If the enterprise is not a success then the entrepreneur either tries again or does something different. Intrapreneurs do exactly the same, but with one difference – they operate with an existing organization. They are looking for ways to create their vision within an existing organization, rather than starting from scratch. It's not necessarily easier or harder than being an entrepreneur, just different.

It has long been realized that individuals want and need more from work than just a salary cheque. Creating an organizational climate in which all employees can function as intrapreneurs is not only very fulfilling for many employees, it is also very positive for the organization. An example of an organization which adopts this approach is the Alhambra Theatre in Bradford. It is very much a tripartite organization: there is a core of administrative and marketing staff; performances are contracted out to the different theatrical, dance and music companies; and there is a pool of temporary staff who work part time in the bars and front of house. Although on paper there is a formal management structure, and clearly-defined job roles, in practice staff take on as much responsibility as they feel able to. Each member of the backstage crew, for example, takes it in turn to co-ordinate everyone's work for a particular show, a role traditionally reserved for the stage manager. One of the members of the backstage staff – a role which is sometimes described as 'moving props around' – has a particular interest in the overall direction of the theatre, and is a key member of the theatre's strategic planning group. In this capacity he may represent the theatre to funding bodies and outside agencies. The Alhambra does not believe in rigid departmental divisons either, so one of their recent sell-out successes, a series of performances by a Dutch dance company, was suggested and organized not by their artistic programmer but by a member of the administrative staff. The staff of the Alhambra believe that this climate of intrapreneurship – also called empowerment – is one of the key reasons why the theatre has one of the best reputations of any regional theatre.

Of course not everyone wants to be an intrapreneur; some people do come to work simply to perform a clearly specified task and receive a fair salary each month. However, in most organizations there are many people who would like more responsibility and freedom of action. Quality Improvement does not mean everyone is obliged to be an intrapreneur, but rather that those who would like to take on this role have the opportunity to do so. This change of thinking from managers and staff to a group of intrapreneurs doesn't mean that organizational hierarchies will automatically disappear. While different people will continue to have different amounts of power and responsibility, the basis of this power will be different. In many organizations today power is derived from position and formal authority. Increasingly in the future, organizational power will derive from expertise, information and interpersonal skills. This too has its dangers. In the same way that the tripartite organization runs the risk of creating an underclass of casual part-time workers, so this emphasis on expertise, information and interpersonal skills runs the risk of creating an underclass of people without these abilities. Education and training have a vital role to play here and will be even more important to Quality Improvement than to TQM.

Implementing Quality Improvement

We have briefly considered in this chapter three aspects of Quality Improvement: its ethical base, its commitment to all stakeholders, and the notion of employees as intrapreneurs. How is this new philosophy to be implemented? Many of the principles of change management described in chapter 4 apply equally to Quality Improvement. People must be ready for change; the strategy should aim to convince a small group of early adopters before addressing a mass audience; and the style of change employed by leaders should make appropriate use of both inflexible, autocratic and flexible, democratic approaches. However, some aspects of change management need special emphasis in the light of the changing nature of both organizations and Quality Improvement.

TQM is often presented as a package; a solution for many, if not all organizational problems. As we have seen, it often fails to deliver. There are many situations in which TQM cannot provide the solution. Quality Improvement goes one step further still; it recognizes that no single package can ever be the solution to all organizational problems. Organizations are inherently very complex entities. Any single management theory, or approach to organizational development, is almost bound to be inadequate in the face of the complex challenges facing most organizations. Unlike TQM, Quality Improvement does not purport to be the answer. It is merely a collection of techniques, some of which might be useful to some organizations in some circumstances. The consequences of this is that Quality Improvement should never be introduced as an organization-wide initiative; instead individuals and teams should adopt whatever aspects of it seem appropriate to them at the time.

When organizations introduce TQM the main thrust of the implementation plan is to try to get other people to change their attitudes and behaviour, often by exhortation rather than example. I explained in chapter 3 that the role of the quality council in TQM was to draw up a statement of values and methods – a quality policy – and prepare a strategy for implementing it; in other words to think how they can change everyone else in the organization. Quality Improvement will take a simpler, but more challenging route. The emphasis will be on changing one's own behaviour, not other people's. The quality council for a Quality Improvement initiative would publish no policies or statements, but would put a great deal of effort into examining and developing the attitudes and behaviour of its own members. Paradoxically, this is more likely to influence other people in the organization. In general, others are more likely to be influenced by what we do than what we say.

None of the ideas in Quality Improvement is new; ethical concerns, stakeholder theory, the concept of intrapreneurship all have long pedigrees. What is new is to combine them with some of the tools and techniques of TQM to produce a coherent approach to developing organizations. There is, I believe, a resistance to organizational philosophies which appear too 'nice'; there is a prevalent belief that to be successful in business you must 'play dirty'. I do not believe this to be the case; cheating, dirty tricks, exploitative wage levels, executive perks, poor treatment of local communities and ignorance of environmental concerns may be recipes for short-term gain but they will certainly lead to long-term failure. The final example in this book is of an organization which operates in a very tough and competitive climate, the food industry. It applies many of the ideas I have described as Quality Improvement and it is very successful in commercial terms. It is called Northern Foods.

Quality Improvement in action

Northern Foods consists of 62 different food businesses, ranging from milk and dairy products through biscuits, pizzas and snacks to ready-made convenience foods. The food industry is not an easy one in which to operate. Consumer trends change rapidly, and both supply and demand are often affected by unpredictable circumstances such as the weather, which can double the price of raw ingredients or bring on a huge demand for certain types of food with little warning. It is an intensely competitive business, with both small ambitious new firms entering the market and established multinationals slogging it out for market share. The industry as a whole has been hit hard by the recession of the last few years. Despite these factors, Northern Foods has continued to expand and is one of the most profitable businesses in the industry sector. To what does it attribute its success?

Northern is certainly perceived within the industry as being a very ethical company. Major customers like Marks and Spencer value the honesty and straightforwardness which characterizes their dealings with Northern. There is a climate within the company which promotes integrity and which is developed not through policy statements or edicts but by the behaviour of staff from chairman Chris Haskins downwards. Staff benefits include a profit-sharing scheme, by which all staff of more than four years' standing receive an allocation of company shares. Northern's share price has risen consistently over a number of years, and many employees choose to keep their shares until they retire. Unlike other industries where excess stock can be stored until sold, many foodstuffs have a very short shelf-life. This fact, coupled with fluctuating demand, inevitably puts pressure on food companies to make use of temporary or casual staff. Northern has gone to great lengths to reduce the use of truly casual staff and to employ temporary and part-time staff on shift patterns which suit the individual as well as the company. With operating companies across the UK employing 31,000 staff in all, Northern Foods is an important part of many local communities. Whenever the opening or closure of a factory is considered by the board, the effect on the local economy is carefully considered, especially if that factory is the main employer in that locality. The company has recently piloted secondments of its staff to work with voluntary groups. This has proved popular both with the local communities, and with Northern staff, and there are plans to extend the scheme. Northern's approach to social responsibility includes making substantial donations to charities such as Oxfam and Save the Children Fund.

At the heart of Northern's approach to business is its attitude towards employees. Throughout the company, there is a strong belief in giving staff as much autonomy as possible. This philosophy is applied at all levels in the organization. The bakers at Fox's biscuits are not subject to examination by quality controllers as are their counterparts in many similar firms; shopfloor workers take full responsibility for the quality of their work. General managers of the operating companies are not subject to bureaucratic group policies or detailed scrutiny from a large head office. Instead they are given full autonomy to run their businesses as they see fit. This belief in autonomy is reflected in the structure of the company. The overall structure of the company is a very flat one. The head office at Hull is very small and rarely gives instructions to individual operating companies; instead a small group of head office staff spends most of their time travelling out to operating companies to advise and influence. Most of the communication between the members of this group takes place in very informal meetings at the beginning and end of each week; Northern Foods generally tries to avoid bureaucratic ways of communicating in favour of informal, face to face communication.

Although many of the practices I have described here are consistent with the Quality Improvement approach Northern Foods would certainly not describe itself as having a Quality Improvement policy. As a company it shies away from policy documents and statements of company philosophy; it believes change is brought about by senior staff acting in a certain way, rather than producing bureaucratic statements which exhort the rest of the company to perform. It is also wary of any management approach which is suggestive of a 'quick fix'. Since it was founded in 1938 as Northern Dairies, the company has always focused on long-term development. As the group personnel executive, Phil Ward, put it to me: 'Any of our general managers could go into one of the other's factories and improve this year's profits. But what about investment for next year, or the year after? We're more interested in long-term growth than in quick fixes.' Northern Foods is not a complacent company; it recognizes there are many areas it still needs to develop. For example, many of its materials are supplied by farms whose use of pesticides has a questionable impact on the environment. As the market currently stands, it would not be possible for Northern to use only organically produced ingredients. These issues are debated, both within the company and with their customers; if there is a trend towards more organically produced food, Northern will be in an excellent position to meet this need. Self-analysis and self-criticism are very much part of Northern's approach.

The future of quality

Predicting the future is a hazardous business; the only thing you can be really sure of is that your predictions will never be 100 per cent accurate. Nevertheless, there do seem to be some aspects of organizational life over the coming years which appear to be very likely indeed. Organizations will be under increasing pressure to perform, to delivery quality. Competition in the private sector will increase, as the flexibility of new, small organizations increasingly threatens large, well-established ones. Public sector organizations, previously largely immune from competition, are now exposed to it as they are privatized or as services are contracted out. Local authorities in particular seem destined to be less providers and more enablers and givers of contracts. Even in the social welfare sector there is a change from grant-giving to charities to a contract culture where voluntary agencies receive money in exchange for the delivery of very specific, quality-rated services. Alongside this growing pressure to deliver quality, it seems certain that organizations, and the context in which they operate, will continue to grow more complex. As I have briefly outlined in this chapter, not only will the organizational forms become more complex, but there will simply be much more to take into account when making a business decision. The nineteenth-century pit owner didn't need to know much about business strategy or management information systems; he simply ordered his men to get the coal out of the ground as cheaply as possible, and then strove to sell it to his local purchaser at as good a price as possible. His contemporary counterparts have to consider political factors, employment legislation and good practice, environmental factors, and the logistics of both national and international markets, to mention but a few.

In the face of pressure to deliver in complex situations, people who lead and work in organizations have a need for guidance, a set of tools and techniques which they can draw on. TQM provides this but has some significant moral and practical drawbacks. However, TQM does form a basis for the emerging body of knowledge called Quality Improvement. Quality Improvement is not a panacea – no single set of techniques could provide all the answers for the complex problems faced by organizations – but it does provide an important set of tools for organizations of the 21st century.

Further Reading

Philip Atkinson, *Creating Culture Change: The Key to Successful Total Quality Management*, Gower 1992.

Phil Crosby, *Quality is Free*, McGraw-Hill 1979.

W. E. Deming, *Quality, Productivity and Competitive Position*, MIT 1982.

Jacques Horovitz and Michele Panak, *Total Customer Satisfaction*, Pitman 1991.

John Knotter and James Hesketh, *Corporate Culture and Performance*, Free Press 1993.

John Oakland, *Total Quality Management*, Heinemann 1989.

Tom Peters, *Thriving on Chaos*, Macmillan 1988.

Barry Popplewell and Alan Wildsmith, *Becoming the Best*, Gower 1988.

Frank Price, *Right First Time*, Gower 1985.

Lynda King Taylor, *Quality: Total Customer Service*, Century Business 1993.

Edgar Willie, *Quality: Achieving Excellence*, Century Business 1993.

Index